Deer

Law and Liabilities

Deer

Law and Liabilities

Charlie Parkes and John Thornley

SWAN·HILL
PRESS

Copyright © 2000 Charlie Parkes and John Thornley

First Published in the UK in 2000
by Swan Hill Press, an imprint of Airlife Publishing Ltd

British Library Cataloguing in Publication Data
A catalogue record for this book
is available from the British Library

ISBN 1 84037 096 3

Typeset by Phoenix Typesetting, Ilkley, West Yorkshire
Printed by WBC Book Manufacturers Ltd, Bridgend, Glamorgan

Swan Hill Press
an imprint of Airlife Publishing Ltd
101 Longden Road, Shrewsbury, SY3 9EB, England
E-mail: airlife@airlifebooks.com
Website: www.airlifebooks.com

Dedication

Steven Beale & Ken MacArthur, B.E.M., F.B.D.S.
Without their friendship and encouragement this book would not
have been written.

Acknowledgements

Dr Tony Mitchell-Jones, English
Nature;

Michael Smith, Scottish
Landowners' Federation;

Dick Youngson, Deer Commission
for Scotland;

Bill Harriman, Head of Firearms,
BASC;

Chris Probert and Fred Currie,
Forestry Commission;

Peter Watson, Deer Officer, BASC;

Mark Mason, Royal Ulster
Constabulary;

Norma Chapman;

David Barnes, Lloyd-Barnes
Solicitors, Ipswich;

Tony Slate and Paul Ramsbottom,
Derbyshire Constabulary;

Peter Lord, Solicitor, Derbyshire
Constabulary;

Abby Turner; Data Protection
Officer, Derbyshire Constabulary;

Stewart Scull, Game and
Gamekeeping Officer, BASC;

Tom Bowler, DHSS Belfast;

John Milburne, DoE Belfast;

Barry Urton, HSE;

Mike Wellman, Cheshire
Constabulary;

Christopher Borthen, *Stalking
Magazine*;

Tom Brown, Northern Ireland
Deer Society;

Chris Jackson, Countryside
Alliance;

Ian Grindy, North West Water;

Dr Joachim Algermissen;

John Adams;

Keith Taylor;

Gerald Barry;

Richard Prior;

G.Kenneth Whitehead;

Sian Mosely, Derbyshire
Constabulary;

Tony Chapman, Derbyshire
Constabulary;

Adrian Evans, Derbyshire
Constabulary;

LACOTS;

British Deer Farmers' Association;

National Game Dealers'
Association;

British Wild Boar Association;

British Deer Society

Eaton Hall · Chester

Since time immemorial deer have been treasured both as a source of food and as a sporting species. In more recent times they have also been recognised for their aesthetic value. They are our largest wild mammal and many people find pleasure in seeing them in the countryside. Their treatment by man has not always been humane and even today they are poached by ruthless gangs who have no respect for deer or the law.

Despite the pressures of poaching and our diminishing green belt, deer continue to increase and extend their range. In doing so, conflicts of interest have arisen. Their presence is not always welcome and although it can be beneficial to our natural environment, it can also be detrimental. Deer damage agricultural crops and can destroy young trees and thereby suppress woodland regeneration. In some areas they are a serious threat to road safety. Hence in many areas their numbers have to be controlled.

These issues increasingly focus on the legal implications of the welfare of deer, public safety and maintaining a balance with economic activities and environmental conservation. This book is devoted to explaining the law and liabilities involved and I am confident that its practical application will be a significant contribution to the welfare of deer and of immense value to all who have an interest in them.

THE DUKE OF WESTMINSTER OBE TD DL

Preface

by the

Chairman of the Deer Initiative

This is an easily understood book that will be valued by all with an interest in deer. Of particular use to landowners, occupiers, and deer managers alike, it brings together all aspects of legislation and legal implications involving deer.

Beginning with the status of deer in our countryside, it also covers their conservation throughout these islands. Regrettably, while deer are exceptional animals to observe, they are, when in large numbers, damaging to the environment and to many of man's interests.

The main part of the book is devoted to laws relating to the control of deer and prevention from abuse. Included is dealing in venison, the use of firearms, trespass and poaching. The section on liabilities is a salutary reminder for all.

This is a welcome contribution to responsible deer management. It fully supports the Deer Initiative mission 'to ensure the delivery of a sustainable, well managed wild deer population in England', and will help to ensure that the mission is accomplished with due regard to the law. I am confident it will be of equal use to those who operate in the remainder of the British Isles.

ANDREW HOON

Contents

CHAPTER 1

Deer – Legal Status and Ownership

There are now over a million wild deer in the United Kingdom, apparently more than at the time of the Norman Conquest. Wild deer, especially our native red and roe deer, are an integral part of our natural and cultural heritage. They contribute significantly to the economic life of much of rural Scotland, especially in the more remote areas of the Highlands. Within an ever decreasing rural landscape the presence of deer adds a most appealing dimension to our way of life and view of the countryside. They are, after all, our largest wild land mammals and the opportunities for seeing them in their natural habitat are now greater than ever.

Historically, deer have been treasured as a rich source of food and a worthy sporting quarry. They have been hunted, originally for food, since the Stone Age. Royal deer hunts of the fifteenth century were full of pomp, ceremony and extravagance, underlining their status as the quarry of kings. However they have never been 'royal' animals, *regalia minora*.

During the Middle Ages a large number of deer parks were created. The deer were kept for hunting and as a ready supply of meat. It was not until the eighteenth century, however, that deer were seen as having an ornamental value on large country estates, some of which later imported different species from abroad. It was from some of these parks and estates that our non-indigenous species such as fallow and subsequently muntjac and Chinese water deer escaped and bred, eventually being recognised as 'wild'.

SPECIES AND DISTRIBUTION

Six species of deer now exist in the wild. They include our native red and roe deer together with the introduced fallow, sika, muntjac and Chinese water deer.[1] A herd of reindeer exists in the Cairngorms of Scotland, but these are privately owned and should not be classed as wild deer.

Since 1850 deer numbers and their distribution have increased substantially. It has been estimated that red deer numbers in Scotland doubled between 1963 and 1969. There are several explanations, but a major factor is the increase in suitable habitat, mainly forestry planting. This has, in some areas, both reduced the traditional red deer range and provided additional habitat for deer of all species. (The twentieth century saw an increase from 4 to 6 per cent in England alone of woodland cover.) In addition, with the extinction of the wolf, adult deer no longer have any natural predators.

Roe deer have substantially increased their range throughout England and the spread of muntjac following releases and escapes from many locations has been dramatic. Sika deer have also continued to spread, increasing concerns for the purity of the indigenous red deer, with which they can interbreed.

DEER SOCIETIES AND ASSOCIATED BODIES

There is now a wide range of organisations with interests in deer, some of which are elaborated upon below.[2]

The British Deer Society (B.D.S.)

The Society was formed in 1963 from a deer group within the Mammal Society, and has branches, each with its own council, covering the British Isles. The British Deer Society is a registered national charity with a charter to promote the welfare of deer. This is achieved by:

---

1. See chapter 7 for identification of each species.
2. See page 203 for address and contact details.

- technical advice to government, organisations and the public on deer management, legislation and conservation
- funding and practical support for research projects
- training novice stalkers and deer managers
- education to all age groups about the importance of deer in our environment

The Society is now based at Fordingbridge, Hampshire, and publishes the magazine *Deer* for its members.

The Northern Ireland Deer Society

The origins of the Society lie in the Ulster branch of the Irish Deer Society, which became an independent body separate from the British Deer Society in 1975. Its aims and objectives are compatible with those of the British Deer Society, which it may soon rejoin to become the Northern Ireland Branch.

The Deer Initiative

In 1995 the Forestry Commission brought together a wide range of statutory and voluntary bodies and private interests to form the Deer Initiative. The partnership aims to promote a co-ordinated approach to the sustainable management of wild deer and to explain the need for the management and methods used to all people with an interest in deer. An independent chairman, reporting to the Forestry Commissioners, was appointed in 1998. At the time of writing (1999), proposals are being considered for the appointment of a national deer management co-ordinator to support the continued growth and development of the Deer Initiative.

The Deer Initiative's objectives and statement of intent are detailed on page 12.

The Deer Commission for Scotland

Formerly known as the Red Deer Commission this statutory body was established in 1959. It has powers to promote the sustainable management of deer, including advising deer managers on the conservation and control of deer and authorising action outside the general framework of the close seasons to protect against deer damage to agriculture and forestry (see chapter 3).

The British Association for Shooting and Conservation (B.A.S.C.)

Formerly the Wildfowlers Association of Great Britain and Ireland (W.A.G.B.I.) B.A.S.C. is Britain's largest country shooting organisation. It provides a wide range of support for those who enjoy shooting sports, many of whom are actively involved in deer management. Of particular note is the assistance available in respect of legal representation and access to expert witnesses for court cases relating to firearms. In 1995 B.A.S.C. appointed a full-time deer officer to pioneer their commitment to supporting members in areas specifically relating to deer. B.A.S.C. is now a representative body for deer stalkers and deer managers and is taking a leading role in setting standards and training qualifications.[3]

The Countryside Alliance

In 1997 the British Field Sports Society, the Countryside Movement and the Countryside Business Group merged to form the Countryside Alliance. One of its aims is to promote, protect and preserve traditional country sports and related activities. Regional and county branches of the Alliance are governed by committees and most have a stalking representative for their area. Deer management in the West Country, where red deer are still hunted with hounds, is strongly supported by the Alliance, which strives to protect the interests of those involved and the welfare of the deer.

The U.K. Association of Professional Deer Managers (U.K. A.P.D.M.)

Formed in 1998 to protect the interests of those engaged in deer management as a profession, the Association's aims are:

- to enhance the standards and maintain the integrity of the deer-stalking profession
- to gain and maintain the confidence of landowners and their agents
- to gain and maintain the confidence of client stalkers

The Association has the full support of the British Deer Society. Its members are subject to a code of practice which should ensure integrity and a high standard of deer management.

---

3. See chapter 7 for stalking competency qualifications.

The British Deer Farmers' Association

In addition to our wild deer there is a considerable number of captive deer in deer farms, parks or private estates. Deer farming has increased in recent years as venison has become a popular meat, particularly following the BSE crisis in beef cattle. The British Deer Farmers' Association, which also covers Northern Ireland, was formed in 1978 to further the interests of deer farmers. It is a nationally accepted body representing deer farming to government departments and the public and private sectors. One of its objectives is to maintain and improve the welfare of deer on enclosed land.

The National Game Dealers' Association (N.G.D.A.)

The N.G.D.A. was founded in 1979 with the primary object of safeguarding and promoting the general commercial interests of members, encouraging best practice throughout the industry and promoting the consumption of all types of game and venison. Membership is open to all licensed U.K. game dealers and processors and to retail licensed game dealers. A code of good handling practice is available through the association.

LEGISLATION

Deer, whether they be wild or captive, have always created conflicts of interest in terms of both their management and their potential as sporting species. Where such conflicts exist, the law has an important role in safeguarding their welfare. Complaints often arise from overpopulation causing crop and environmental damage. A fine balance therefore exists between deer numbers and the need to protect the natural heritage. Stalking, whether professionally as a means of control or for sport, is strictly regulated by the firearms legislation which is elaborated upon in chapter 6.

History

Through the ages, various provisions have been made by Act of Parliament for the protection of deer with grave penalties for those who broke the law. The Normans did much to develop the forest laws that applied to large tracts of countryside to ensure that there were sufficient deer to be hunted by the nobility and to provide for the royal table. Many of the older statutes were repealed by the Larceny Act, 1861. This Act, which was replaced by the Theft Act, 1968, created specific offences of taking deer from both forests and deer parks together with offences of illegal possession of carcases or poaching equipment. The legislation only covered unauthorised taking and did not protect deer from being treated like vermin – being killed indiscriminately, regardless of breeding season, using totally inadequate firearms.

Now, at the turn of the twenty-first century, extensive legislation exists to protect deer of all species, wild and captive, safeguarding their welfare in matters relating to humane methods of killing, poaching and the provision of close seasons to preserve the species. However, variations exist between the law in England and Wales, Scotland and Northern Ireland.

The legislation on which this book is based is not exhaustive and loopholes exist. It will also be appreciated that matters affecting deer, and those who manage them, are diverse. Consequently a wide cross-section of legislation, outside that specifically relating to deer, is involved.

The Main Acts relating to deer

The principal legislation providing protection for deer is as follows. In England and Wales it is the Deer Act, 1991, which provides protection for deer of any species and includes the carcase of any deer or any part thereof. Venison is defined separately.[4]

The Deer (Scotland) Act, 1996, provides protection for deer as specified, i.e. fallow, red, roe, sika and any other species of deer specified by order of the Secretary of State. It includes the hybrids of

4. See chapters 2 and 5.

those species (currently red and sika) and, where appropriate, the carcase of any deer or any part of it.[5] The legislation for Scotland, where deer contribute significantly to the rural economy, has over the years sought to bring about a more purposeful move towards deer management via the powers of the Deer Commission.

In Northern Ireland the protection for deer is provided in Part III of the Wildlife (Northern Ireland) Order, 1985. The Order relates to any deer with the exception of offences relating to close seasons in respect of fallow, red, sika or any hybrids of these species. The sale and purchase of venison is regulated under Article 23.[6]

OWNERSHIP AND RIGHTS TO TAKE WILD DEER

Wild deer that are free to roam from one person's land to another belong to no one; they are ownerless. They are wild animals, *ferae naturae*, and therefore are known as *res nullius*, things without an owner.[7]

Ownership of the land which wild deer may occupy does not carry with it any rights of ownership of the deer whilst they remain wild. However, the Common Law has always conveyed to the landowner certain rights in respect of the use of the land and things found upon it. Consequently deer found dead on the land, caught accidentally in fences or killed in some other way become the property of the landowner, subject to any legal agreement in which the rights may have passed to another – e.g. in a sporting lease.

Who owns cast antlers?

5. See chapter 3.
6. See chapter 2.
7. The Case of Swans 1592 -Co.Rep.15b at 17b.

It is suggested that the ownership of cast antlers is also vested in the owner of the land on which they fall and that someone removing them without authority may be liable if the matter were disputed. Similarly, the ownership of deer killed in road accidents passes to the owner of the land upon which the collision has occurred. This will normally be the adjacent land owner rather than the highway authority. However, the driver has no claim on the land owner in cases involving wild deer regardless of whose land they were on immediately prior to the collision. The driver has no legal right to retain the deer carcase.

The spread and increase of wild deer in the U.K. have led to serious national concern not only for road safety but also for the conservation and welfare of the species involved. The problem is not merely restricted to a few counties with high densities of deer. Accidents involving deer pose a significant risk of human injury and damage to vehicles and is closely correlated to the size of the species concerned. Reliable statistics for the U.K. relating to accidents involving deer are not available; road traffic legislation does not require the mandatory reporting of such accidents to the police unless someone other than the driver involved is injured.[8] Research for the Highways Agency, however, suggests there are 30,000–50,000 road accidents involving deer annually in the U.K., and that up to 400 people are injured and 10 killed as a result.

Considerable research has been undertaken into methods designed to prevent deer-related accidents. Whilst some have had a measure of success, only full-height deer fencing has been found to significantly reduce accidents. Civil litigation may in the future be pioneered in areas of new development in which the highway authority has not adequately safeguarded road users from the dangers caused by deer.

A number of issues have arisen from dealing with deer casualties, including response schemes, legal requirements for firearms,[9] humane methods of dispatch,[10] dealing with the public and disposal of carcases. A code of practice is being developed by B.A.S.C.

Theft

Originally wild deer were not regarded as property at Common Law or under the Larceny Acts and therefore they could not be stolen in

---

8. The Road Traffic Act, 1988, requires road accidents involving horses, asses, mules, cattle, pigs, sheep, goats and dogs to be reported to the police in certain circumstances.
9. See chapter 6.
10. See chapter 7.

any circumstances whilst they remained wild. However, the Theft Act, 1968, now recognises them as 'property' and defines the circumstances in which they may be stolen.

Section 1(1) of this Act provides:

> A person is guilty of theft if he dishonestly appropriates property belonging to another with the intention of permanently depriving the other of it; 'thief' and 'steal' shall be construed accordingly.

Section 4(4) provides:

> Wild creatures, tamed or untamed, shall be regarded as property; but a person cannot steal a wild creature not tamed nor ordinarily kept in captivity, or the carcase of any such creature, unless either it has been reduced into possession by or on behalf of another person and possession of it has not since been lost or abandoned, or another person is in the course of reducing it into possession.

As a general rule with regard to wild deer, theft will only be committed if they are taken after they have passed into someone's possession or constructive possession, e.g. where deer have been shot or captured for some reason in circumstances where they are confined in an area where they have no means of escape. There will be situations in which it will be clear that the deer are 'property belonging to another' and where they have been 'reduced into possession or are in the process of being reduced'. The most obvious are deer that have been shot and are in the process of being taken off the hill *en route* to the larder or venison dealer. A person taking a carcase without authority in this situation, say from an argocat or trailer, will commit theft if the intention is to permanently deprive the owner of it.

Wild deer caught-up, kept in deer farms or held in securely fenced parks for whatever reason are reduced into possession and therefore clearly capable of being stolen. However, if they escape it may be said that 'possession has been lost or abandoned', in which case a subsequent unauthorised taking will be poaching rather than theft. As discussed later in respect of 'captive' deer, it is unlikely that possession would be abandoned in circumstances where the deer are not wild or were clearly identifiable as such.

The overall effect of this legislation is that deer, whilst in their wild state – free to roam where they please – cannot be stolen. It would make no difference if the deer were caught-up and ear tagged then released back into the wild or indeed if they were tended during the winter months by supplementing their feeding. A similar situation exists with the tagging of reared or caught-up pheasants that are then released into the wild and fed by a gamekeeper. Deer can, of course, be poached and the laws described in chapter 9 provide protection, not only for the deer, but also for the landowner's rights described earlier.

The Theft Act does not apply in Scotland although the Common Law offence of theft in Scotland imposes similar criteria.

Sporting rights

Traditionally the rights of owners of land have included the exclusive right to kill and take wild animals on their land,[11] subject of course, to the laws that protect those animals and any legal agreement to the contrary e.g. where the sporting rights to the deer have been let. These rights are known in law as 'incorporeal hereditaments' and may be extended to an occupier or anyone else by licence. It should be noted that where the rights to take deer have been reserved by the landowner, or have been let to a third party, the occupier will have a right to take deer only if acting on their authority.

Agricultural tenants do not normally acquire the sporting rights to their holdings automatically by virtue of their agricultural lease and often the sporting rights will have been reserved by the landlord. If they are not then the rights do transfer with the possession of the land to the new tenant.[12] This is not the case in Scotland where the right is considered as personal to the owner of the land.[13]

In England and Wales an occupier or tenant who suffers serious crop damage by marauding deer can take action outside the close season but this does not convey any independent rights to kill the deer over and above that of the owner. In this situation deer of the same species causing the damage could only be shot by the occupier or tenant if they had a legal right to kill the deer – i.e. they hold the sporting rights themselves or have the authority of the landowner or person with the sporting rights to the deer. In Scotland the tenant has an absolute right to protect crops by killing deer.[14]

Are deer game?

Deer should not be classed as game or described as such. Historically the Game Acts never included deer within such a definition and when the intention has been to include deer within legislation affecting

11. Blades v. Higgs 1865. 11 H.L.Cas.621.
12. Pochin v. Smith 1887 52 J.P.4; Anderson v. Vicary 1900.
13. Saunders v. Pitfield 1888. 58 L.T.108.
14. See chapter 4.

game they have been specifically referred to. In Scotland it has been conceded by the Crown that 'game' in the Game (Scotland) Act 1832, does not include deer and the court has held that the inclusion of deer was not a tenable construction of 'game' when the history of the 1832 Act was examined.[15]

The fact that in certain circumstances i.e. on unenclosed land,[16] a licence to kill game is required to take deer can be misleading. The Game Licences Act, 1861, which makes this provision, does not include deer within the definition of game but lists them separately together with woodcock, snipe and rabbits.

In England and Wales deer were not seen as a traditional sporting species to the same extent as in the Highlands. Sporting rights and leases mainly relating to game would rarely specify deer and it was common for deer to be excluded in the wording of deeds. However this was challenged in 1987 by the Inglewood Investment Company who owned the sporting rights to 1000 acres of Cannock Chase in Staffordshire. The company sought a declaration that the Forestry Commission was not entitled to kill deer on the estate. A deed of 1921 was referred to which reserved the rights to 'all game' and it was contested this included deer. The case was eventually decided in the Court of Appeal. Dismissing the company's appeal, Lord Justice Dillon sitting with Lords Justices Butler-Sloss and Staughton said the word 'deer' was 'conspicuous by its absence' in terms of the deed which reserved sporting rights to Lord Hatherton over 'all game, woodcock, snipe and other fowl, hares, rabbits and fish'. Lord Justice Dillon said that in legislation when deer were meant to be included they were expressly mentioned and when they were not specified they were taken to be excluded. He rejected the company's argument that deer should be included because they were animals fit for food and usually sported after.

It is advisable therefore that sporting rights to take deer should be specific in terminology and actually refer to deer. Use of the word 'game' is not accurate or sufficient. Deer are not game as described earlier and such reference may lead to uncertainty and dispute as to whether deer were ever intended to be included in the rights. We would go even further and suggest that the document should include the species or simply specify 'any deer'. Such rights should be in a written form of licence and signed. These should be detailed and accurate in respect of the area of land over which the right exists and ideally incorporate a map. Provisions as to licence fee and periods

15. Ferguson v. Macphail 1987 SCCR 52.
16. See chapter 7.

of notice can also be included, together with the right to take away deer once they have been killed. It is desirable that such licences be drafted by a lawyer familiar with the subject.

The Management of deer and statutory rights

In addition to those who possess the right to take deer by virtue of land ownership or sporting rights, legislation exists in Scotland to ensure that owners of land take appropriate action to control deer numbers. In cases where they do not the Deer Commission is given certain rights within the Deer (Scotland) Act, 1996, to kill deer over and above the rights of the owner.[17] However, no opposing legislation exists anywhere in the country to protect a species from culling to the point of extinction. There are no legally binding management controls and consequently landowners, if so minded, are entitled to exterminate every deer on their land provided they comply with the existing law governing seasons and permitted methods of taking. This is not the case in other parts of Europe where regional controls can be enforced in terms of the maximum number of deer culled.

This is clearly a most unsatisfactory situation in terms of both the future welfare of our wild deer and their effective management, on which many other species of flora and fauna depend.

The Deer Initiative has now been formed with the following Statement of Intent:

> Deer are our largest land mammals and are an important part of our natural environment. People enjoy seeing deer in the countryside and they have value as a conservation resource and as a traditional sporting quarry.
>
> Because man's modification of the environment has increased feeding opportunities for deer and eliminated their predators, populations can rise to the point where they may cause serious damage to trees, agricultural crops and conservation interests.
>
> In areas where the landscape provides good conditions for deer, management may be necessary to ensure that deer numbers are held at a level that is in balance with economic activities and environmental conservation.
>
> The Deer Initiative recommends that deer management is based on a careful study of deer numbers, their habits and their impact. It should be carried out in a planned way over long periods and not simply in response to specific problems.

17. See chapter 3.

The management of deer should be carried out, wherever possible, by considering whole populations. As these generally cover several land ownerships, land managers should co-ordinate their activities through Deer Management Groups.

Where deer numbers must be reduced, shooting by rifle is the most humane method currently available. Shooting should be carried out by skilled and trained stalkers, with human safety and the humane treatment of the deer as the overriding priorities.

Wild deer have increased in numbers and range throughout England in the past thirty years and the need for management is increasing too. The Deer Initiative aims to promote informed responsible management and to explain the need for management and methods used to all people with an interest in deer.

The following objectives, if successful, will go a long way towards achieving a more co-ordinated approach to deer management in England:

- to build consensus amongst partners and produce and endorse consistent and balanced advice
- to raise the awareness of the public, politicians, central and local government, policy-makers and all land managers of the need for a co-operative and co-ordinated approach to deer management
- within a co-ordinated network of Deer Management Groups to assist with the formation of local deer-management strategies
- to promote best practice with regard to safety, humaneness, monitoring and research
- to promote a responsible approach towards deer stalking within a framework of sustainable population management
- to encourage a stable venison market
- to encourage effective woodland design for deer management
- to address the problems associated with deer and roads
- to encourage sound deer management training
- to identify research, survey and monitoring needs
- to exchange and disseminate information
- in advice and promotion, to be sensitive to the considerable public interest in deer

Capture and handling

Many of the traditional methods of capturing deer, the origins of which go back thousands of years, involve catching them alive, usually as a prelude to their slaughter for food and clothing. Pits, snares, spear traps and many other devices, now illegal, have been used to kill or immobilise deer. Methods over the years have changed although, as described in chapter 10, immense cruelty is still involved in modern-day poaching.

The use of pits is no longer considered safe or effective, although netting is still an important technique of physical capture, particularly for small and medium-sized deer. The use of drugs to immobilise large animals such as deer is long established and derives from the use of curare-like substances obtained from the bark of trees in the Amazon basin. Considerable research during the twentieth century has been undertaken and has led to the development of new weapon systems and drugs. Effective and relatively safe drugs that can be delivered in a variety of ways now enable deer to be temporarily immobilised. However the use of drugs is not a technique that can easily be applied to wild deer, especially in woodland. It is therefore more appropriate for use in zoo, park and farm situations.

The capture and handling of wild deer is now controlled by legislation. This provides, under appropriate licence, for their capture and handling in circumstances which would otherwise be illegal due to the method used or time of year. Such circumstances include removing deer from one area to another, or taking deer alive for scientific or educational purposes.[19] In England this is controlled by licence issued by English Nature and for Wales by the Countryside Council for Wales. In Scotland advice should be sought from the Deer Commission. In Northern Ireland licences are issued by the Department of the Environment.

Applicants for such licences are required to specify full details of their aims and purpose in taking deer alive, together with the species, number and sex. The method of capture and the applicant's experience in handling deer or other large animals must also be stated. Where the use of stupefying drugs or muscle-relaxing agents are intended, their use should be justified. The type of drug and dosage for each species together with the weapon to be used must be given.

Careful consideration is given to such applications and licences are issued only if all conditions are satisfied and the purpose justified. Where licences are granted they are subject to whatever conditions are considered appropriate for the particular circumstances. For example they may include carrying and producing a copy of the licence to a police officer on demand, guidelines on the safe and humane handling of live deer to be followed, close supervision of equipment used to take or transport deer, the fact that deer should be immobilised for as short a period as possible and kept under super-

19. See chapter 2.

vision until fully recovered, and the submission of a report after the operation to the issuing authority.

Under the firearms regulations[20] Home Office authority must be obtained before using dartguns and blowpipes. There are also statutory constraints on the possession, supply and administration of certain drugs; questions about possession and supply should be directed to the Home Office Drugs Branch. Queries concerning the administration of such drugs should be directed to the Ministry of Agriculture, Fisheries and Food, Animal Health Division III.[21]

Hunting with hounds

The hunting of deer with hounds may be viewed as a legitimate management control method of capturing deer to enable their humane dispatch or simply for the sport of the chase. Until 1963 the 'carted' stag or hind involved captive deer being released from a trailer and then hunted purely for sport, often to be recaptured at the end of the hunt and placed back in the cart. Hunting wild deer with a pack of hounds is still practised in southern England and Ireland, but is illegal in Scotland.

Deer movements are studied by a person known as a 'harbourer', who will locate a suitable beast and report back to the Master at the meet. In ancient times the fumes (deer droppings) would be brought back in a hunting horn to the Lord who would then consider whether the beast was worthy of hunting. Modern hounds are built for stamina rather than speed and consequently the hunt may take several hours. When at bay the deer is humanely shot. Over the years there have been a number of incidents involving court action against hunts. They have often involved trespass and cruelty claims, some of which are elaborated on in chapter 7.

It remains a matter of great controversy as to whether the hunting of deer with dogs should be allowed to continue. Research undertaken by Professor Bateson[22] into the levels of stress suffered by hunted deer raised the debate as to whether this was acceptable. As a consequence some large landowners like the National Trust have declined to give permission for hunting on their land.

20. See chapter 6.
21. See page 205 for contact details.
22. See Bibliography.

CAPTIVE DEER

Throughout the ages deer have been exploited and domesticated. Archaeological evidence exists from China and Europe to suggest that they may have been partially domesticated many centuries before the Romans and Greeks confined their deer to walled or fenced areas. Many of the deer were kept for the purpose of providing venison and so the idea of deer farming was born many years ago.

Theft

Deer that are tamed or in captivity are deemed under the Theft Act, 1968, as being property capable of being stolen and therefore anyone taking them without authority or permission would commit a theft, as defined earlier. Deer rustling is not common, perhaps because the fencing is more secure than that used for other livestock. Where deer are taken from the wild without authority the offence is poaching rather than stealing.[23]

In circumstances where deer are suspected of being stolen, proof of ownership would be required, but difficulties arise in the identification of unmarked deer. Deer kept in deer farms should be conspicuously marked so that they can be identified. This is normally done by an ear tag linking the deer to the owner. Photographs may prove useful, particularly if a beast has a distinguishing feature, which is more likely with the male of the species through antler identification but may not always be conclusive.

Some years ago an interesting case arose in Derbyshire in which a captive red deer stag was taken during the night from within a securely fenced area in the park of a stately home. It was quickly noticed the following morning that the beast was missing. A subsequent search of the area revealed half the carcase hidden away in the undergrowth.

Observations were mounted by the police and park warden on two consecutive nights but to no avail. The carcase was therefore removed. On the third night a van was seen in the vicinity by the warden. It looked suspicious and he alerted the police. It was later stopped some miles from the park and searched. To the officer's surprise, venison was found in the rear together with a hacksaw.

When interviewed the driver said the meat had been purchased as dog meat from an unknown man in a lay-by near a local market town. As for the cutting equipment, this had only been used for cutting metal. Forensic scientists were able to prove that within the teeth of

23. See chapter 9.

the saw were fragments of bone. Needless to say the magistrates did not believe the man's story and they convicted him of handling stolen property since it could not be proved he was involved in the original theft. Nowadays, forensic scientists could put the case beyond doubt by the analysis of DNA samples linking the venison left behind with that found in the van.

If captive or tame deer have escaped they remain the property of the owner, unless the owner has abandoned rights to them, and anyone taking them without authority would be stealing them. However if the taker believed them to be wild, it would be difficult to secure a conviction unless it was shown the person knew they were tame or from captive stock. Clearly if the deer were easily identifiable as belonging to captive or tame stock such a defence would be weakened. Irrespective of the taker's culpability in these circumstances and provided identification could be satisfactorily made, title in the carcase would remain with the original owner.

Deer of a species not generally accepted as being 'wild' in this country should be readily identifiable as belonging to someone. For example if an elk appeared whilst you were waiting in your high seat you would have difficulty in proving you considered the beast to be wild and ownerless. Clearly it would be reasonable to assume this was someone's property and any taking of the animal would be theft. If shot, a more appropriate charge may be criminal damage.

An elk in this country would not be considered wild and ownerless.

Reindeer in Scotland

The reindeer in the Cairngorms and Glenlivet in Scotland pose an interesting case. Incidents have occurred in the past in which their status has had to be considered. Some view them as wild, others as captive or tame. The herd, approximately 130 strong, is privately owned and was established in 1952. Over fifty beasts are free ranging in an area of 6000 to 7000 acres on the northern slopes of the Cairngorms. They are a tourist attraction and a support scheme exists in which individual reindeer can be 'adopted'. The animals are domesticated and tame. Under the supervision of a guide the tourist can walk amongst the herd, stroking and feeding them. Some of the animals are tagged and between the months of April and September they are all herded into a 1000-acre enclosure. We would suggest in the circumstances the animals should not be treated as wild, *ferae naturae*, but in the same way as other livestock on the open hill, i.e. as property belonging to someone. Hence they could be stolen or damaged. Should this issue be disputed it would be for the courts ultimately to decide on the merits of a particular case whether the deer were wild or the property of someone.

Reindeer

The Liabilities of keeping deer

The keeping of animals brings with it responsibilities, not only in terms of the criminal law but also in terms of civil liability. In civil law a distinction is made between two classes of animals – those which belong to a dangerous species and those which do not.

The Animals Act, 1971 (England and Wales) and the Animals (Scotland) Act, 1987, both deal with civil liability involving injury or damage caused by animals. It will be noted that there are some differences between the two Acts. However, generally speaking owners of animals that are either regarded as a dangerous species or known to have dangerous tendencies are liable should they damage property or injure someone.

The Animals Act, 1971

Section 2(1) says that where any damage (which includes death of or injury to any person including disease or impairment of mental condition) is caused by an animal which belongs to a dangerous species the keeper of the animal is liable for the damage. A dangerous species is defined as one 'which is not commonly domesticated in the British Islands and whose fully grown animals . . . are likely unless restricted to cause severe damage'.

The Act does not specify which species fall within this category. The majority of these animals are of a type more likely to be kept in zoos or safari parks. Many species will clearly fall into the class of 'dangerous', e.g. lions or tigers, but both camels and elephants have been held to be dangerous.[24]

There are no species of deer specified in the Dangerous Wild Animals Act, 1976,[25] which makes provision for licensing control in the interests of public safety and nuisance. However the Act will apply to deer of any species if the circumstances fall within the criteria detailed in section 1(2) below:

Where damage (or injury) is caused by an animal which does not belong to a dangerous species a keeper of the animal is liable if:

(a) the damage is of a kind which the animal, unless restrained, was likely to cause or which, if caused by the animal, was likely to be severe; and

(b) the likelihood of the damage or of its being severe was due to characteristics of the animal which are not normally found in animals of the same species or are not normally so found except at particular times or in particular circumstances; and

(c) those characteristics were known to that keeper or were at any time known to a person who at that time had charge of the animal . . .

24. McQuaker v. Goddard 1940 1KB.687. and Filburn v. People's Palace and Aquarium Co. Ltd. 1890 25QBD.258. respectively.
25. Wild boar, however, are included.

A 'keeper' of an animal is defined as someone who owns the animal or has it in their possession.

The Animals (Scotland) Act, 1987

> A person is liable for any damage or injury caused by an animal if:
>
> (a) at the time of the injury or damage complained of, he was a keeper of the animal;
>
> (b) the animal belongs to a species whose members generally are by virtue of their physical attributes or habits likely (unless controlled or restrained) to injure severely or kill persons or animals, or damage property to a material extent; and
>
> (c) the injury or damage complained of is directly referable to such physical attributes or habits.

It follows therefore that as owner or person in charge of an animal you may be liable if someone is injured or damage is caused if it can be shown that you had knowledge of a certain animal's unnaturally harmful tendencies and that no action had been taken to prevent such an occurrence. This would apply to captive deer, particularly roe bucks for example that are potentially dangerous at certain times of the year and red deer during the rut.

There have been many cases taken to court, some of which have set precedents, but there is an important Common Law principle which the courts are willing to apply in such cases, involving the ordinary duty of care as set out in the case of Fardon v. Harcourt-Rivington 1932 as:-

> Quite apart from the liability imposed upon the owners of animals or the person having control of them by reason of knowledge of their propensities, there is the ordinary duty of a person to take care either that his animal or chattel is not put to such a use as is likely to injure his neighbour – the ordinary duty to take care.

Exceptions to liability exist under both Acts and cover situations where it can be shown that the injury or damage caused is due to the fault of the person suffering it, or that they had voluntarily accepted the risk thereof or that at the time they were trespassing.

As is so often said in legal matters, the courts will make judgements on the merits of a particular case and will take account of judgements and cases stated.

CRUELTY

Legislation exists to protect deer from acts of cruelty, whether they be wild or captive. However, the law is much stronger in respect of the latter. The circumstances in which offences of cruelty to wild deer may be committed in England, Wales and Scotland are covered in chapter 7.

Captive deer kept for the production of food, skin or antlers fall within the definition of 'livestock' and animal welfare legislation exists to protect them from being caused unnecessary pain and distress. All domestic and captive deer are additionally protected against acts of cruelty under the Protection of Animals Act, 1911 (England and Wales), the Protection of Animals (Scotland) Act, 1912, and the Welfare of Animals Act (Northern Ireland) 1972.

The Agriculture (Miscellaneous Provisions) Act, 1968 and Welfare of Animals Act (Northern Ireland) 1972 says in Part I, section 1:

> Any person who causes unnecessary pain or unnecessary distress to any livestock [this includes deer as defined earlier] situated on agricultural land and under his control or permits such livestock to suffer any pain or distress of which he knows or may reasonably be expected to know commits an offence.

The term 'agricultural land' is defined as land used for agriculture within the meaning given by the Agriculture Act, 1947. This gives a wide interpretation which includes livestock breeding and keeping, grazing and meadow land and the use of land for woodlands where that is ancillary to the farming of land for other agricultural purposes.

Regulations made under section 2 of the above Act include the Welfare of Livestock (Prohibited Operations) Regulations, 1982, as amended.[26] These regulations covering England, Wales and Scotland prohibit certain operations on animals situated on agricultural land, in particular (Paragraph (xii)) the removal of any part of the antlers before the velvet is frayed and the greater part of it has been shed. The regulations do not apply to any act lawfully done under the Animals (Scientific Procedures) Act, 1986,[27] to the

---

26. Welfare of Livestock (Prohibited Operations) (Amendment) Regulations, 1987. SI 1987/114.
27. This Act provides for a system of licensing control of experimental and other scientific work carried out on living animals.

rendering of first aid in cases of emergency, or to the performance of operations by a veterinary surgeon for the proper treatment of disease or injury.

In Northern Ireland the Welfare of Animals Act (section 14) prohibits any operation which is performed without due care and humanity or which involves interference with the sensitive tissues or bone structure without the use of anaesthetic. Exemptions exist which include minor operations by veterinary surgeons, tail docking and castration.

The Protection of Animals Act, 1911, the Protection of Animals (Scotland) Act, 1912 (these acts may be cited together) and the Welfare of Animals Act (Northern Ireland) 1972 state:

Section 1(1)

Ill-treatment:

(a) It is an offence to cruelly beat, kick, ill-treat, over-ride, over-drive, torture, infuriate or terrify any animal, or to cause the animal any unnecessary suffering by wantonly or unreasonably doing or omitting to do any act.

Persons who cause, permit or procure such acts also commit the offence.

Transportation

(b) It is an offence to cause an animal unnecessary suffering by the manner in which it is conveyed or carried.[28]

Fighting and baiting

(c) It is an offence to cause, procure or assist at the fighting or baiting of any animal or to keep or use premises for the purpose.

Poison and drugs

(d) It is an offence to administer any poisonous or injurious drug or substance to any animal.

Operations

(e) It is an offence to subject any animal to an operation which is performed without due care and humanity.[29]

Dehorning (Northern Ireland only)

It is an offence to use rubber bands or any other form of constriction for the purpose of dehorning any animal.

---

28. Additional offences may be committed under the Transport of Animals (General Order) 1973.
29. See page 21 Animals (Scientific Procedures) Act, 1986.

Abandonment

A cruelty offence is also committed under the Acts as follows:

If a person having charge or control of any animal abandons it, permanently or not, without reasonable cause or excuse, in circumstances likely to cause the animal unnecessary suffering.

The Protection of Animals Acts, 1911 and 1912 were amended by the Abandonment of Animals Act, 1960, to include this provision, which is also contained in the Act relating to Northern Ireland.

It has been held that it is impossible to say whether an animal has been abandoned without considering the length of time that it had been left. The question of the owner's intention on leaving the animal is of some relevance. Where an owner has made or attempted to make arrangements for the animal's welfare, he could not be said to have abandoned it.[30]

Explanatory notes and exemptions

The 1911 Act was a consolidating Act and amalgamated previous legislation. The phraseology relating to cruelty can be seen as unnecessarily confusing and the terms overlapping, and this has been commented upon by the High Court. In referring to the policy underlying the legislation one judge commented that it was high time the law was expressed in clear, intelligible modern language.[31]

An owner shall be deemed to have permitted cruelty by failing to exercise reasonable care and supervision in respect of the protection of the animal. The words describing the acts of cruelty create separate offences.

The expression 'animal' means any domestic or captive animal. 'Domestic animal' includes farm animals, as defined in the Act, together with dogs, cats or fowl, or any other animal whatever the species which is tame or which has been or is being sufficiently tamed to serve some purpose for the use of man.

'Captive animal' means any species of animal, bird, fish or reptile which is in captivity or confinement or which is maimed, pinioned or subjected to any appliance or contrivance for the purpose of hindering or preventing its escape.

The legislation in Northern Ireland refers to *any* animal, which would include those that are wild.[32]

30. Hunt v. Duckering 1993. TLR 23.3.93.
31. Isted v. CPS 1998. 162 JP 513.
32. As to when a wild animal in England, Wales and Scotland may be deemed captive see chapter 7.

Section 1(3)b states that nothing in section 1 shall apply to the coursing or hunting of any captive animal subject to certain conditions. This is elaborated upon in chapter 7.

The courts have decided that the mere infliction of pain for a necessary purpose is not cruelty but that unnecessary and unreasonable abuse of an animal is an offence of cruelty.[33] It is for the courts to decide on the circumstances of individual cases.

33. Ford v. Wiley 1889.

CHAPTER 2

Conservation and Protection in England, Wales and Northern Ireland

In the nineteenth century the legislators' attention was directed mainly at the preservation of game, normally defined as game birds and hares. Deer have never been defined as game but have often been included in the game laws. For example the wording in the Game Licences Act 1860, 'game or any deer', clearly differentiates between game and deer.

Whereas the game laws have remained almost unchanged since 1831, deer legislation was created in 1963 and 1980. The 1963 Act dealt with close seasons, unlawful methods and crop damage. Its failure to address poaching was resolved by the 1980 Act, which made deer poaching a criminal offence, controlled the sale of venison, and gave the police powers to enforce the 1963 and 1980 Acts and the courts powers to confiscate deer, weapons, equipment and vehicles. Unlike other poaching legislation and the fisheries law in particular, there was, and remains, no power of arrest by landowners or occupiers.

The Deer Act 1991 consolidated the two Acts and several

amendments contained in various other Acts. It also made some minor wording changes to the deer legislation. In this Act deer mean deer of any species and includes the carcases or any part thereof. The Act makes some exceptions for farmed deer.

POACHING

Section 1(1) of the Act states:

> It is an offence, without the consent of the occupier, owner or other lawful authority, to enter any land in search or pursuit of any deer with the intention of taking, killing or injuring it.

Section 1(2) states:

> It is an offence, without the consent of the occupier, owner or other lawful authority, while on any land, to:
>
> (a) Intentionally take, kill or injure any deer or attempt to do so.
>
> (b) Search for or pursue any deer with any such intent, or
>
> (c) Remove the carcase of any deer

But under section 1(3), the person will not be guilty under (1) or (2) above if:

(a) he believed he would have had the owner's or occupier's consent, if he/she had known of the circumstances, or

(b) he believed he had a lawful authority

These offences are discussed in greater detail in chapter 9.

TRESPASS BY A HUNT

Section 35 of the Game Act 1831 provides that the offences of daytime poaching will not apply to persons hunting or coursing on any land with hounds or greyhounds, if in fresh pursuit of deer, hare or fox already started on other land. This is covered further in chapter 8.

CLOSE SEASON

Under section 2(1) it is an offence for anyone to take or intentionally kill any deer listed in Schedule 1 (currently red, fallow, roe or sika) during the close season. It is also an offence under section 5 to attempt to commit the offence.

CLOSE SEASONS

Red Deer	All dates inclusive
Stags	1 May to 31 July
Hinds	1 March to 31 October
Fallow Deer	
Buck	1 May to 31 July
Doe	1 March to 31 October
Roe Deer	
Buck	1 November to 31 March
Doe	1 March to 31 October
Sika Deer	
Stags	1 May to 31 July
Hinds	1 March to 31 October

Red/sika hybrids are not included in the Schedule and it could be argued that the close season does not apply. Conversely it can also be argued that a hybrid is a form of red or sika and is covered by the close season. There is no answer to this point until a case is decided by the courts, who may follow the example in Scotland where hybrids are included.

Whilst there is no statutory close season for muntjac and Chinese water deer the recommended close seasons are:

Muntjac	
Male	1 May to 31 July
Female	None realistic due to breeding cycle
Chinese Water Deer	
Male or female	1 March to 31 October

There are several exceptions which allow the taking of deer in the close season. Under section 2(3), the close seasons do not apply to the killing of conspicuously marked farmed deer enclosed within a deer-proof barrier where deer are kept, by way of business, for breeding, meat or other foodstuffs, skins or other by-products. The killing must be done by the farmer, or his/her servant or agent.

Conspicuously marked farm deer.

Taking deer at night

Under section 3 it is an offence to take or intentionally kill deer of any species at night (i.e. between one hour after sunset to one hour before sunrise). It is also an offence under section 5 to attempt to commit the offence.

Exceptions to close seasons and night close times

Prevention of suffering

Under section 6(2) it is not an offence under sections 2 or 3 relating to close seasons and night close times to kill or take a deer to prevent its suffering if injured or diseased. In such circumstances a trap or net, normally prohibited by section 4(1)(a)(b), may also be used, but not poison.

Humane dispatch

Section 6(4) permits the use of any shotgun and ammunition for the dispatch of a deer which has been so seriously injured, otherwise than by the unlawful act of the dispatcher, or was in such a condition that to kill it was an act of mercy.

A typical example would be a stalker or keeper called out to deal with a road casualty. The exception is not applicable to the person who commits any unlawful act which results in the deer being injured.[34]

In Scotland mercy killing is any act done for the purpose of preventing suffering by an injured or diseased deer or by any deer calf, fawn or kid deprived, or about to be deprived, of its mother.[35]

Prevention of damage
Deer could also be killed during the close season and at night under section 98 of the Agriculture Act 1947 to prevent damage. This exception would require the issue of a specific order from the Ministry of Agriculture.

Scientific purposes
Section 8 provides for the issue of licences to take or remove deer for scientific or educational purposes, thereby exempting the holder from sections 2 to 4.[36]

UNLAWFUL WEAPONS

The poacher's arsenal is a mixture of modern and medieval technology, ranging from infrared sights, light-intensifying devices, four-wheel-drive vehicles and sophisticated firearms to the crossbow, snare and hunting dog.

Traps, snares, poison and nets

Under section 4(1)(a) it is an offence to set in position any trap, snare, poisoned or stupefying bait so placed as to be calculated to injure any deer coming into contact. Under section 4(1)(b) it is an offence to use any trap, snare, poisoned or stupefying bait or any net to kill or take any deer.

Firearms, bows and arrows, and drugs

Under section 4(2)(a), it is an offence to use any of the following to take, kill or injure any deer:

- a rifle less than a .240 or with a muzzle energy less than 2305 joules (1700 ft/lb)

---

34. The use of firearms and other methods are discussed in chapters 6 and 7.
35. See chapter 3.
36. See chapter 1.

- a rifle bullet other than soft or hollow nosed
- an air weapon
- a smooth-bore gun or cartridge for such

A deer may be killed with any smooth-bore gun if it is seriously injured or in such a condition that to kill it would be an act of mercy; but one would have to show that the injury was not caused by one's own unlawful act. An unlawful act is any offence under any Act and could include the use of a rifle without a certificate or whilst poaching.[37]

A smooth-bore gun may be used as a slaughtering instrument if it is not less than 12 bore, has a barrel less than 24 inches and is loaded with AAA shot or larger. This kind of weapon is carried by deer hunts and, because of the short barrel, requires a firearms certificate.

Under section 4(2)(b)(c), it is an offence to use any of the following to take, kill or injure any deer:

- an arrow, spear or similar missile
- missiles, whether discharged from a firearm or otherwise, containing a poison, stupefying drug or muscle relaxant

The Wildlife and Countryside Act 1981 prohibits the use of a bow or crossbow to kill or take any animal.

Motor vehicles

Under section 4(4), it is an offence to discharge a firearm or project any missile at any deer from a powered vehicle (e.g. car, boat, aircraft, helicopter or hovercraft) or to use such a vehicle to drive deer. It is also an offence under section 5 to attempt to commit these offences. Under section 4(5) such actions are not illegal, however, if carried out by, or with the written authority of, the occupier of any 'enclosed land where deer are usually kept, and in relation to deer on that land'.

As far as we are aware, there is no case law to guide us in relation to the interpretation of the section. The Deer Act does not define the wording. However in the Deer (Scotland) Act 1996, 'enclosed' means 'enclosed by stock-proof fence or other barrier'. It does not define 'enclosed land where deer are usually kept'. Jemmison v. Priddle 1971 gave a ruling on 'enclosed land' in relation to an

---

37. See chapter 6 on the use of rifles and handguns for humane dispatch.

exemption within the Game Licensing Act, 1860. For the purposes of this Act this was taken to mean land enclosed by normal agricultural hedges as opposed to moorland where no enclosures existed.[38]

Historically similar wording can be traced back to the Larceny Act, 1861 (now replaced by the Theft Act, 1968). Section 13 related to offences of taking deer in 'any inclosed land where deer shall be usually kept'. The purpose of the section would appear to be to protect what were viewed then as 'wild deer' in large parks or forests that were walled or fenced. The Common Law provided protection for other deer that were considered 'tame'. Section 15 of the Act made it an offence unlawfully and wilfully to destroy any part of any fence on land where 'deer are usually kept'. This tends to suggest that the areas were deer-proof and the deer therein captive.

In our opinion the wording 'inclosed land where deer are usually kept' implies the land is used for such a purpose and would warrant deer-proof boundaries.

Attempts to commit offences and possession of equipment

It is an offence under section 5 to attempt to commit any offence under sections 2–4. It is also an offence to possess for the purpose of committing an offence under section 2 or 4:

i. An article prohibited under sections 4(1)(b), 4(2)(b) or (c) above, or
ii. Any firearms or ammunition

EXCEPTIONS FOR OCCUPIERS AND AUTHORISED PERSONS

Under section 7(4) an authorised person is:

* the occupier of the land on which the action is taken
* a resident member of the occupier's household authorised in writing by the occupier
* a person in the occupier's service (e.g. an employee) authorised in writing by the occupier
* a person having the right to take or kill the deer or a person authorised in writing by him (e.g. a shooting tenant, gamekeeper and guests)

38. See chapter 7.

Crop damage

If deer are causing serious damage, under section 7(1)(2) and subject to the conditions laid down in section 7(3), an authorised person may:

- take or kill the deer by shooting during the close season on cultivated land, pasture or enclosed woodland
- use a smooth-bore gun to kill the deer on any such land, at any time, if it is not less than a 12 bore and is loaded with AAA shot or a single non-spherical bullet, not less than 22.68 grammes (350 grains), commonly known as a rifled slug

However, the authorised person must be able to show that:

- there was reason to believe that deer of the same species were causing, or had caused damage to crops, vegetables, fruit, growing timber or any other form of property on the land
- it was likely that further serious damage would be caused
- the action was necessary to prevent it

This exemption provides a loophole in that some farmers plant crops close to woods or land containing deer with the intention of attracting them through an open gate or broken-down fence onto the land.

Where an authorised person takes action against marauding deer to protect crops etc., the killing must take place on the land where the damage is occurring, and not the land where the deer come from.[39] Chapter 4 deals with crop damage in more detail.

39. See the case of Traill v. Buckingham in chapter 4.

MOVING AND RELEASING DEER

Under section 8, English Nature can grant a written authority in the form of a licence which exempts an individual from offences under sections 2, 3 and 4 (close season, night and prohibited methods). The purposes of such a licence are to remove deer from one area to another or to take deer alive for scientific or educational purposes. The Countryside Council for Wales can issue licences under the same conditions.

The licence can approve the use of any net, trap or missile containing a stupefying drug or muscle-relaxing agent. Each application is treated on its merits and is normally assessed by the regional offices prior to the licence being issued by the head office.

Under section 14(1) of the Wildlife and Countryside Act, it is illegal to release or allow to escape into the wild any animal which:

(a)   is of a kind which is not ordinarily resident in and is not a regular visitor to Great Britain in a wild state; or

(b)   is included in Part 1 of Schedule 9 [includes sika and muntjac].

ENFORCEMENT

Enforcement by authorised person

For the purpose of enforcement, an authorised person is the owner or occupier of land or someone authorised by them or having the right to take or kill deer on that land. If such an authorised person reasonably suspects that someone is or has been committing offences under section 1(1)(2) (poaching) they may require the person to give their full name and address and quit the land forthwith. There are no powers of arrest and no guarantee that any name given is genuine. At best such action may only scare the poacher off the land but your objective may be achieved. There is little chance of a prosecution unless the police are involved, who may use their general powers of arrest under the Police and Criminal Evidence Act.

Failure to comply with such a request is an offence, but only a police officer has the power of arrest or the means of obtaining the name or address if it is refused. The owner or occupier or their employee may treat the suspected person as a trespasser and eject them from the land using reasonable force.

If a police officer stops a vehicle containing a carcase the officer will not know if the deer is wild or from a deer park or farm. In such cases the officer could initially treat the situation as one of theft until the ownership or otherwise of the deer is established. Where deer are considered to be captive, tamed or domestic (e.g. farmed deer or deer enclosed in a deer park), they may be classed as property; in which case the offence of theft under the Theft Act, 1968 may be committed and a citizen's arrest made.[40]

Enforcement by the police

Under section 12, the police are given additional powers of enforcement. A police officer who reasonably suspects that someone is or has been committing any offence under the Act may enter any land (but not a dwelling house), and, if he or she suspects that evidence may be found, may without warrant:

- stop and search the suspect
- search or examine any vehicle, animal, weapon or other thing
- arrest the suspect under the Police and Criminal Evidence Act 1984 general arrest conditions
- seize and detain anything that is evidence or liable to be confiscated by the court
- sell deer or venison and retain the proceeds until the case is decided at court

Forfeitures and disqualification

On conviction the court may order the confiscation of:

- deer or venison in respect of the offence or found in the person's possession
- any vehicle, animal, weapon or other thing used to commit the offence, or which was capable of being used to take, kill or injure deer and was found in their possession

For offences under sections 1, 10, 11 and 13(3)(c) the court may also disqualify a person from holding a game dealer's licence and cancel his/her firearm or shotgun certificate.

---

40. See chapter 9 p.185.

PROTECTION AND CONSERVATION IN NORTHERN IRELAND

Deer protection in Northern Ireland is covered by Part III of the Wildlife (Northern Ireland) Order, 1985, which is substantially similar to the Deer Act, 1991.

Except where otherwise provided, 'deer' means deer of any species and their hybrids, and includes those on enclosed land where deer not in the wild state are usually kept. The Order makes some exceptions for farmed deer.

Close season

Under Article 19(1) it is an offence for anyone to take or intentionally kill any deer listed in Schedule 10 during the close season (i.e. red, fallow or sika). Hybrids of these species are included in the Schedule. It is also an offence under Article 5 to attempt to commit the offence.

CLOSE SEASONS

Red Deer	All dates inclusive
Stags	1 May to 31 July
Hinds	1 March to 31 October
Fallow Deer	
Buck	1 May to 31 July
Doe	1 March to 31 October
Sika Deer	
Stags	1 May to 31 July
Hinds	1 March to 31 October

There are certain exceptions, which are explained below.

Taking deer at night

Under Article 19(2) it is an offence to take or intentionally kill any deer at night (i.e. between one hour after sunset to one hour before sunrise).

Firearms

Under Article 19(3)(a) and Schedule 11 it is an offence to use any of the following to take, kill or injure deer:

- a rifle less than a .236 or with a muzzle energy less than 2305 joules (1700 ft/lb)
- A rifle bullet other than a bullet not less than 100 grains (6.48 grammes) or an expanding bullet designed to deform in a predictable manner and thereby increase its effective diameter upon entering tissue
- any air weapon
- any smooth-bore gun or cartridge for such
- any weapon which discharges a missile by gas propellant
- any form of handgun other than a slaughtering instrument[41]

Under Article 19(3) it is an offence for any person to discharge a firearm or project any missile from a mechanically propelled vehicle at deer (this does not apply to anything done by, or with the written authority of, the occupier of enclosed land where deer not in the wild state are usually kept, in relation to deer on that land)

Removing, transporting and marking deer

Under Article 19(4) it is an offence for any person to –

(a)   take and remove any live deer;
(b)   mark, or attach any tag, ring, collar or other device to any live deer; or
(c)   use aircraft to transport live deer (except inside the aircraft).

41. Article 2(2) Firearms (Northern Ireland) Order, 1981.

Exceptions

Article 20(2) specifies that nothing in Article 19 shall make unlawful:

- anything done by a vet when treating deer; or
- in relation to 19(1) close seasons; 3(b) shooting from a vehicle; or (4)(a)(b) taking or marking live deer, anything done by, or under the direction of, a person certified by the Department of Agriculture who keeps and breeds deer by way of business, in the course of business; or
- any act done to protect a person immediately endangered by deer on enclosed land where deer not in a wild state are usually kept, if the act is reasonable in the circumstances.

Another exception involves crop protection (see chapter 4 for more detail), and Article 20(7)(b) permits the use of any shotgun and ammunition for the dispatch of a deer which had been so seriously injured, otherwise than by the unlawful act of the dispatcher, or was in such a condition that to kill it was an act of mercy. A typical example would be a stalker or keeper called out to deal with a road casualty. The exception is not applicable to the person who commits any unlawful act which results in the deer being injured.

Poaching

Article 22(1) states it is an offence, without the consent of the occupier, owner or other lawful authority, to enter any land in search or pursuit of any deer with the intention of taking, killing or injuring it. Under Article 22(2), it is also an offence, without the consent of the occupier, owner or other lawful authority, while on any land, to:

- Intentionally take, kill or injure any deer,
- Search for or pursue any deer with any such intent, or
- Remove the carcase of any deer.

But under Article 22(3), the person will not be guilty under (1) or (2) above if:

- he reasonably believed he would have had the owner's or occupier's consent, if he/she had known of the circumstances, or
- he has other lawful authority to do it.

These offences are discussed in greater detail in chapter 9.

Unlawful weapons

Article 12 prohibits the use of self-locking snares, bows, crossbows, arrows, spears and sound recordings to kill or take any wild animal including deer.

Red, fallow and sika deer are also included in Schedule 6 of the Order which further prohibits the use of:

- traps and snares
- drugs and poison
- automatic or semi-automatic firearms
- a metal bar, hammer or similar
- a device for illuminating a target or night-sighting device
- an artificial light, mirror or dazzling device
- gas or smoke

In addition the use of a mechanically propelled vehicle in immediate pursuit of such deer for the purpose of driving, killing or taking them is an offence.

Movement and release of deer

Article 21 allows for licences to be granted by the Department of Environment for scientific and educational purposes or for removing deer from one area to another.

Article 15 prohibits the release or escape into the wild of any animal which:

- is of a kind not ordinarily resident in and is not a regular visitor to Northern Ireland in a wild state or
- is included in Part 1 of Schedule 9

The release of red, fallow or sika requires a licence from the Department of Environment and the release of other species would be illegal.

Enforcement and penalties

Enforcement by authorised person

For the purpose of enforcement, an authorised person is the owner or occupier of land or someone authorised by him or having the right to take or kill deer on that land. Under Article 22(5) if such an authorised person reasonably suspects that someone is or has been committing offences under Article 22(1)(2) (poaching) he may require the person to give his full name and address and quit the land forthwith. There are no powers of arrest and no guarantees that any name given is genuine. At best such action may only scare the poacher off the land but your objective may be achieved. Failure to comply with such a request is an offence.

Enforcement by the police

Under Article 25, the police are given additional powers of enforcement. A police officer who reasonably suspects that someone is or has been committing any deer-related offence under Part III of the Order may enter any land (but not a dwelling house), and, if he suspects that evidence may be found, may without warrant:

- stop and search the suspect
- search or examine any vehicle, animal, weapon or other thing
- arrest the suspect using general arrest powers under Article 27 of the Police and Criminal Evidence Act
- seize and detain anything that is evidence or liable to be forfeited by the court; deer and venison must be produced to a court which may order it to be sold, destroyed or liberated

A search warrant can be granted in respect of offences under Articles 19 and 23.

Forfeitures and disqualification

Under Article 27(7) on conviction the court:

- shall order the confiscation of deer or venison in respect of which the offence was committed; and
- may confiscate any vehicle, animal, weapon or other thing used to commit the offence.

For offences under Articles 1, 10, 11 and 13(3)(c) the court may also disqualify a person from holding a game dealer's licence and cancel his/her firearm or shotgun certificate.

CHAPTER 3

Conservation and Protection in Scotland

The legislation covering the protection of deer in Scotland is the Deer (Scotland) Act, 1996 and a number of Orders made under previous Acts:

- the Deer (Firearms etc.) (Scotland) Order, 1985
- the Deer (Close Seasons) (Scotland) Order, 1984
- the Licensing of Venison Dealer (Application Procedures etc.) (Scotland) Order, 1984
- the Licensing of Venison Dealer (Prescribed Forms etc.) (Scotland) Order, 1984

The Act is divided into four parts:

- Part I, The Deer Commission for Scotland
- Part II, conservation, control and sustainable management of deer
- Part III, unlawful taking and killing
- Part IV, dealing in venison and enforcement

The species in Scotland are red, fallow, sika, roe and red/sika hybrids, which may explain the conditional definition of deer in the Act: 'deer' means fallow, red, roe and sika and any other species specified by the Secretary of State, and includes any hybrid of those species and, where appropriate, 'the carcase of any deer or any part of it'. In our view the last phrase appears to cater for venison dealing and poaching.

The Deer Commission has issued a Policy for Sika Deer in Scotland because of their ability to cause considerable damage to woodland and hybridise with the native red deer. Although sika deer are covered by the legislation, they are an alien species living in the wild, and further releases or movements are banned. Any attempt to introduce muntjac is also prohibited. Under section 14(1) of the Wildlife and Countryside Act, it is illegal to release or allow to escape into the wild any animal which

(a)   is of a kind which is not ordinarily resident in and is not a regular visitor to Great Britain in a wild state; or

(b)   is included in Part 1 of schedule 9 [includes sika and muntjac].

The basis of the legislation is that deer may only be taken or killed by shooting in the daytime during the open season. Obviously, such strict criteria would cause many problems for farmers and occupiers of land, so the law allows for culling in specified circumstances.

PART I: THE DEER COMMISSION FOR SCOTLAND

The Deer (Scotland) Act 1996 consolidated the provisions from the Deer (Scotland) Act 1959 which established the Red Deer Commission. The change of title in 1996 to the Deer Commission for Scotland was accompanied by a change of remit to include: the sustainable management of deer; damage to the natural heritage, agriculture or woodlands; deer welfare; and deer which are causing a danger to the public. The remit was also extended to include fallow, roe and sika.

The Commission advises the Secretary of State for Scotland and the Scottish Parliament on any deer-related matter, has the power to advise landowners regarding open hill management, woodland deer and stocking and culling levels, and is able to support and assist in research.

On a more general basis, it co-ordinates the different interests of

41

land managers for the benefit and more effective management of an important wildlife resource. It considers the broad problems of land use, the effects of forestry planting programmes, the natural heritage, legislation and scientific research on deer in Scotland. The Commission is a statutory consultee of the Forestry Commission and advises private individuals and companies on forestry grant schemes and forestry protection.

Land below the 450-metre contour is in great demand for a number of uses, especially forestry; and in order that all interests are protected, deer control carries a high priority. In this respect it is vitally important to balance numbers with available winter range. Deer managers have a responsibility to minimise the risk of deer damage and cannot expect farmers and crofters to overwinter their deer; consequently the law makes provision for agricultural occupiers to protect their crops. The annual culls of red deer in 1996–7 and 1997–8 were 61,482 and 61,627 respectively.

The Commission needs information to carry out its functions. Under section 40 it can require occupiers to provide returns of the numbers of deer killed on their ground. Occupiers include tenants or sub-tenants, whether in actual occupation of the land or not. Failing to supply the information is an offence. Section 42 also calls for the occupier of agricultural land or enclosed or unenclosed woodland to supply the owner of the land with the number, sex and species of deer killed in the preceding twelve months.

Farmed deer

Under section 43, apart from the exceptions below, the Act does not apply to farmed deer, which are deer of any species kept as livestock on agricultural land and enclosed in a deer-proof barrier. The exceptions are:

- killing otherwise than by shooting when slaughtered in the field
- the use of a firearm which is not approved
- venison dealing

PART II: CONSERVATION, CONTROL AND SUSTAINABLE MANAGEMENT OF DEER

Close seasons

Under section 5 and the Deer (Close Seasons) (Scotland) Order, 1984, no person shall take or wilfully kill or injure specified deer in the following close seasons:

Species	male	female
Red deer, sika deer and red/sika hybrids	21 October–30 June	16 February–20 October
Fallow deer	1 May–31 July	16 February–20 October
Roe deer	21 October–31 March	1 April–20 October

Section 5(5) stipulates that it is an offence to take, wilfully kill or injure deer during the close season unless certain exceptions apply. This includes attempts and preparatory acts to kill deer. The Deer Commission has powers to adjust the close seasons in certain locations to meet seasonal conditions.

These dates were fixed for both welfare and sporting purposes but, in the case of red deer particularly, mainly on humanitarian grounds. Stags are usually well run after their exertions during the rutting season towards the end of October. And hinds are heavily pregnant by spring and have dependent calves at foot after mid-June. A close season must be set for females of every species but *may* be set for males.

It should be noted that the Deer Commission is not a policing authority and the decision to prosecute remains with the police and procurator fiscal.

Under section 5(6), the Deer Commission can authorise the owner, occupier or a person nominated in writing by either of them, to take or kill and sell deer during the close season if necessary for the following reasons:

(a)
    (i)   to prevent serious damage to unenclosed woodland or the natural heritage generally, or
    (ii)   in the interests of public safety; and
(b)   no other reasonable means of control are adequate in the circumstances.

Natural heritage includes fauna and flora, geological or physiological features and the natural beauty and amenity of the countryside.[42]

The Commission may also authorise the taking of deer for scientific purposes.

---

42. See chapter 4 for more on crop protection.

Control agreements

Competing with livestock for food.

Section 7(1)(a) states:

> Where deer on any land have caused, are causing or are likely to cause:
>
> (i) damage to woodland, to agricultural production including crops or foodstuffs, or directly or indirectly to the natural heritage generally; or
>
> (ii) injury to livestock (includes farmed deer) by serious overgrazing of pastures, competing with livestock for supplementary feed; or otherwise; or
>
> (b) have become a danger or potential danger to public safety; the Commission can consider measures to reduce the numbers of deer in an area which may include taking or removal of deer from an area. This might include sites of particular economic or conservation value or public places such as the airports.

For the purpose of this section natural heritage includes any alteration or enhancement of the natural heritage which is taking place, or is proposed to take place, either naturally or as a result of change of use determined by the owner or occupier of the land.

Following consultation with interested parties the Commission can draw up a control agreement for the specified area. The agreement will contain the measures to be taken, the number, species, sex and class of deer to be killed, taken or removed, the measures to be taken by owners and occupiers, and time limits.

The Commission is now using voluntary control agreements. It is targeting and agreeing with Deer Management Groups balanced deer populations and target culls, especially of females. Work is also progressing on deer management plans with groups and involving estate staff and owners in thinking carefully about population structures, distribution and impact.

A control agreement may be made in anticipation of future damage, injury or danger, but a control scheme (see below) may only be made where deer have caused, or are causing, serious damage or injury or are and remain a danger to the public, necessitating action.

Control schemes

Under sections 8 and 9 where the Commission cannot secure a control agreement or the agreement is not being carried out they *shall* make a control scheme to prevent serious damage, injury or danger. Such schemes cannot be invoked in the case of altering or enhancing the natural heritage.

A control scheme specifies the measures to be taken by individual owners and occupiers, but they cannot require the erection of a deer-proof fence. If the owner or occupier does not implement the measures the Commission can take the required action and sell the deer taken. Any expenses incurred by the Commission in excess of the proceeds from the sale of the deer are recoverable from the occupier or owner. Aggrieved owners and occupiers may appeal to the Scottish Land Court to vary the amount to be recovered. The Commission may, in a particular case, waive their right to such expenses.

Under section 13, a person who refuses or wilfully fails to comply with a requirement of a control scheme or who wilfully obstructs a person acting under an authorisation issued under Part II commits an offence.

Emergency measures

If the Commission considers that the powers outlined above are inadequate to deal with serious damage, injury or danger it can, under section 10, implement emergency measures. These can include a written request to the person with the rights to take deer on that land to undertake the killing of deer forthwith. If the person is unable or unwilling to comply with the request then the Commission can authorise another person to take the deer. Where the deer constitute a danger or potential danger to the public and shooting such deer may constitute a danger to the public other methods can be approved. Such situations could include deer near airports, railway lines, school playgrounds and parks.

Section 15 allows persons authorised in writing by the Commission to enter land at any reasonable times to exercise functions under section 10. Under other circumstances the power to enter land is permitted following the service of a notice on the owner and occupier.

Other provisions

Persons authorised or required by the Commission to kill deer do not require a game licence (section 38).

Under section 39, without prejudice to sections 8(8), 9, 10(10) and 12(1) the Commission shall have no power to dispose of deer taken under its authority.

PART III: UNLAWFUL TAKING AND KILLING[43]

The basis of the legislation is that deer may only be taken or killed by shooting with the appropriate firearm, in the daytime, during the open season. It therefore prohibits the use of traps, snares, nets, dogs and other methods.

Under section 17 it is an offence:

(i)   Without legal right or permission to take, wilfully kill or injure deer on any land [take means taking deer alive].
(ii)   To remove the carcase of any deer from any land without legal right or permission from someone having such legal right.
(iii)   To wilfully kill or injure any deer otherwise than by shooting [shooting means with the prescribed firearm and ammunition].

There is a view based on the game laws that where deer are legiti-mately shot on land where authority exists, but fall dead over the boundary, they can be recovered. Whilst this may provide a 'legal right' in (ii) above there remains the issues of trespass and ownership of the carcase at civil law.[44]

Night shooting

Under section 18 it is an offence to wilfully kill or injure deer at night. Night is the period between the end of the first hour after sunset to the commencement of the last hour before sunrise. The Commission may authorise persons to take deer at night under the terms of their Code of Practice,[45] notwithstanding anything contained in an agree-

43. Poaching offences are discussed in greater detail in chapter 9.
44. See chapter 7.
45. See pages 55–58.

ment between the occupier and the owner of agricultural land or woodland.

The use of vehicles to drive and shoot deer

It is an offence to use a vehicle to drive deer on any land with the intention of taking, killing or injuring them. The Commission may authorise the driving of deer for the purposes of deer management, which does not include any sporting activity. 'Vehicle' does not include aircraft or hovercraft (section 19).[46]

Under section 20, it is an offence:

- to shoot at deer from a moving vehicle or aircraft
- to use an aircraft for transporting live deer other than in the interior of the aircraft unless done by or under the supervision of a veterinary surgeon or practitioner

The Commission has been demonstrating and evaluating the effectiveness of helicopters in the sustainable management of red deer hinds. The purpose was to demonstrate the use of a helicopter to:

- allow estate stalkers to locate and assess groups of deer prior to a culling operation
- place stalkers in positions that will allow them to stalk deer in a traditional manner and to select and kill cull animals
- follow up the traditional cull operation by summoning the helicopter to recover stalkers and carcases

The Commission is aware of the difficulties being experienced by some estates in reaching their target hind culls. These difficulties include the effects on deer movement of increased culling effort and reduced numbers of estate staff. In addition, short daylight hours during the culling season together with problems associated with access to deer in remote locations has prompted the Commission to consider new approaches.

The Commission hopes to secure agreement to helicopter demonstrations in at least five locations throughout the Highlands of Scotland. It is expected that the helicopter will be used for a period of two to three days at each location. Targets for numbers of deer to be culled during demonstrations are not being set. Estate stalkers will use their professional judgement through selection for culling deer. The cull achieved through deployment of stalkers by helicopter will

46. See pages 52–54 for the Commission's Code of Practice on using vehicles.

be compared to that normally achieved through deployment of stalkers by traditional methods.

The Commission is using helicopters more in carrying out its functions and these demonstration projects follow successful trials of summer population assessments.

Firearms and ammunition

Under section 21, the Secretary of State can specify in an Order the classes of firearms, ammunition, sights and other equipment for the lawful killing of deer. Persons who fail to comply with the Orders commit an offence. The current Order is The Deer (Firearms etc.) (Scotland) Order, 1985.[47]

Under section 21(5) it is an offence wilfully to injure a deer with any firearm or ammunition.

If two or more persons act together to do any act which is an offence under sections 17 to 21 then, according to section 22, each person commits the offence.

Illegal possession of deer

Under section 23 an offence is committed by a person who is in possession of a deer, firearms or ammunition in circumstances which infer that:

1. he obtained the deer by committing an offence under sections 5 or 17 to 22; or
2. he had used the firearm or ammunition for the purpose of committing an offence under sections 5 or 17 to 22; or
3. he knew that:
   (i)   an offence under sections 5 or 17 to 22 had been committed in relation to the deer; or
   (ii) the firearm or ammunition had been used for committing an offence under sections 5 or 17 to 22.

The evidence of one witness is sufficient to charge and convict.

It is a defence to section 23 if the accused can show that no such offence had been committed, or that he had no reason to believe such an offence had been committed.

A person who acts in good faith in connection with the prevention or detection of crime or investigation or treatment of disease does not commit the offence.

47. See the firearms chart on page 101 and chapter 6.

Exemptions for certain acts

Prevention of suffering

Under section 25 an offence is not committed in respect of any act done for the purpose of preventing suffering by an injured or diseased deer or by any deer calf, fawn or kid deprived, or about to be deprived, of its mother. This means that if a doe has been culled, the offspring can also be culled.

A typical example of this exemption would be a stalker or keeper called out to deal with a road casualty. It applies to any person who will undertake the necessary action and in these exceptional circumstances the suffering animal may be dispatched by some means other than shooting with a prescribed firearm.[48]

Crop protection in the close season[49]

Under section 26 it is lawful for a person to take or kill, and sell or dispose of any deer found in the close season on:

(a)   arable land, improved permanent pasture (other than moorland) and land which has been regenerated so as to be able to make a significant contribution to the productivity of a holding which forms part of that agricultural land; or

(b)   enclosed woodland.

where the occupier has reasonable grounds for believing that serious damage will be caused to crops, pasture or human or animal food-stuffs on that agricultural land or to that woodland if the deer are not taken or killed.

The action can be taken by the occupier or the following if they are authorised in writing by the occupier:

- the owner in person
- the owner's employees
- the occupier's employees
- any person normally resident on the land
- any other fit and competent person approved in writing by the Commission

It is conceivable that a particular nominee might be competent to kill deer on the occupier's land if he lawfully held the required

---

48. See chapter 7 for more on humane dispatch.
49. See chapter 4 for more on crop protection.

firearm for the purpose, but might be considered unfit or unsuitable for the purpose by the Commission – for example, a notorious poacher or offender or someone who had otherwise come to adverse notice.

Woodland in this context means not just commercial forestry plantations but any land on which trees are grown, any such trees and also the vegetation amongst the trees on that land. A woodland is enclosed if it is surrounded by stock-proof, but not necessarily deer-proof, fencing or other barriers.

Serious damage is not defined and is a difficult area. It can be qualified in turnip fields, developing corn fields and silage fields but damage to permanent grassland is more difficult to assess. Damage to woodlands at different stages of woodland growth is quantifiable, e.g. browsing of leading shoots and bark stripping. Along with Scottish Natural Heritage the Commission is investigating methods for assessing damage to habitats and the significance of damage. In some communities browsing is beneficial in allowing species diversity.

Nothing contained in an agreement between an occupier and the owner of the land shall prohibit the above lawfully conducted control. However if the landowner or owner of the sporting rights believes that no damage is occurring or likely to occur they can challenge the actions or intentions of the tenant in court (section 26(3)).

Deer may be taken during the close season for reasons other than crop damage but only if such activities are authorised in writing by the Commission.

Use of shotguns

Generally the use of shotguns is neither permitted nor recommended. However the Orders made under the Act do permit the persons listed on page 49 to use specified shotguns and ammunition for crop control as defined in section 26.

The shotgun must be not less than 12 gauge loaded with:

- for shooting any deer, a single rifled non-spherical slug weighing not less than 380 grains (24.62 grams); or a cartridge loaded with SSG or larger
- for roe deer, a cartridge loaded with AAA or larger

PART IV: DEALING IN VENISON AND ENFORCEMENT[50]

Search and seizure

Under section 27,

- a police constable may seize any deer liable to be forfeited on conviction of an offence under the Act
- a sheriff or justice of the peace may grant a search warrant to the police, if satisfied there is reasonable suspicion that an offence under Part III or sections 36(1) or (4) has been committed and evidence of it is to be found on any premises or in any vehicle
- the police authorised by such a warrant, in addition to searching the premises etc., may also search every person found therein or whom they reasonably suspect of having recently left or to be about to enter, and seize any article they have reasonable grounds to believe is evidence relating to the offence
- in cases of urgency the police, having reasonable suspicion that an offence under Part III or sections 36(1) or (4) has been committed, may stop and search without a warrant any vehicle where they believe evidence may be found

Arrest

Under section 28 a police officer may arrest any person found committing an offence under Part III of the Act.

Cancellation of firearm certificates

Section 31(2) states that on conviction for an offence under sections 17–23 the court may cancel any firearm or shotgun certificate.

Cancellation of venison dealer certificate

Under section 31(5), on conviction for an offence under Part III or section 36 the court may disqualify a person from holding or obtaining a venison dealer's certificate.

---

50. See chapter 5 for more on venison dealers.

Disposal of deer

Under section 32, where a deer is seized under the Act and is liable to forfeiture, it may be sold and the net profits will then be liable to forfeiture.

CODES OF PRACTICE

The use of vehicles

Code of Practice on the Use of Vehicles
for the Purposes of Deer Management
Prepared and published by the Deer Commission for Scotland in pursuance of Section 37(5)(b) of the Deer (Scotland) Act, 1996

> Any person issued with an authorisation to drive deer by vehicle is obliged to comply with this Code of Practice. Failure to do so can result in an authorisation being withdrawn.

1. Introduction

The Deer (Scotland) Act 1996 restricts the driving of deer by vehicle, on any land, for the purposes of taking or killing them to those people with written authorisation from the Deer Commission for Scotland.

The Commission may authorise the owner of any land which deer are on, or any person nominated in writing by such an owner, to use any vehicle in circumstances where it may be necessary to drive and take alive or kill deer, during the hours of daylight, for the purposes of deer management. The Commission will require to be satisfied that this method of culling is necessary, that no other method would be appropriate under the circumstances, and that the person authorised is fit and competent for the purpose.

Authorisations are subject to such conditions as may be specified, including the precise area where such work is to be carried out. The Commission will determine when authorisations will be issued for each sex and species of deer and determine the period of their validity.

Firearms safety and the humane dispatch and welfare of deer are paramount in the issue of authorisations for driving deer by vehicle and must be the overriding consideration of operators.

For the purposes of this Code 'deer management' does not include driving deer in the course of any sporting activity; and 'vehicle' does not include any aircraft or hovercraft.

2. Compliance with the following conditions is obligatory

Authorisations issued by the Commission for the driving of deer by vehicle contain the following obligatory conditions and will only be valid if these conditions are adhered to:

2.1 For the killing of RED, SIKA, RED/SIKA CROSSES AND FALLOW DEER, a rifle using ammunition of not less than 6.48 grams (100 grains) soft-nosed bullets, with a muzzle velocity of not less than 746.76 metres (2450 feet) per second *and* a muzzle energy of not less than 2373 joules (1750 foot/pounds), must be used.

2.2 For the killing of ROE DEER, a rifle using ammunition of not less than 3.24 grams (50 grains) soft-nosed bullets, with a muzzle velocity of not less than 746.76 metres (2450 feet) per second *and* a muzzle energy of not less than 1356 joules (1000 foot/pounds), must be used.

2.3 A shotgun may not be used unless specifically authorised by the Commission and in such circumstances the bore and type of ammunition to be used will be specified in the Authorisation.

2.4 Authorisations must be returned to the Commission within 7 days of the date of expiry and include all details of the number, species and sex of deer killed.

3. Situations under which authorisations may be granted

3.1 *Agricultural Areas:* To drive deer which are coming on to crops to an area with a safe backdrop for killing, away from human habitation and domestic stock, where they can be clearly seen and killed.

3.2 *Woodland Areas:* To drive deer which are in woodlands or areas which are being replanted or regenerated to areas with a safe backdrop where they can be clearly seen and killed.

3.3 *Natural Heritage:* To drive deer, for the purposes of management and control in sensitive areas of natural heritage value, to areas with a safe backdrop where they can be clearly seen and killed.

3.4 *Open Range*: To drive deer, for the purposes of deer management and population control, to areas with a safe backdrop where they can be clearly seen and killed.

3.5 *Deer in Public Places:* To drive deer away from areas of potential threat to public safety to adjacent areas where they may be safely removed or killed.

4. Principles and methods

4.1 The local Deer Management Group and other directly affected neighbours should be advised of the proposals.

4.2 A main consideration in driving deer to places where they can be conveniently or more safely shot is to do this with minimum stress to the animals.

4.3   Operators should be familiar with the terrain, behaviour pattern and likely direction of movement of the deer and work must be planned to coincide with their natural daily movement pattern. Care should be taken not to drive deer over unduly rough or difficult terrain where the risk of injury may be high.

4.4   Vehicle operators should remain at reasonable distances from deer being driven to avoid panic and prevent family groups being split up. Deer should not be driven at excessive speeds or over long distances.

4.5   If fences have to be negotiated, sections must be temporarily dropped or gates left open.

4.6   Shooting should only be carried out in areas where there are suitable backstops and care must be taken when shooting one deer not to injure others. Shooting from an elevated position such as a high platform or trailer can enhance the efficiency of the operation. Shooting must not take place from within vehicles.

4.7   Operators should, where possible, refrain from driving groups of female deer during periods of late pregnancy. If it must be done it should be with the minimum stress to the animals.

4.8   Where possible only small groups of deer should be driven to areas where they can be killed and all orphaned calves must be shot during the operation or immediately after the event. The repeated driving of deer on successive days often results in lower levels of success.

4.9   Operators should ensure that deer are standing still and clear of a group at the time of shooting. A heart/lung shot (up to 100 metres for roe and up to 200 metres for larger deer) is recommended. Shooting in excess of these distances should not be attempted. Where the use of a shotgun has been authorised by the Commission, shooting should not exceed a distance of 25 metres for all species.

4.10   Only vehicles that are suitable for the terrain should be used.

4.11   Operators should observe all safety precautions relating to the use of vehicles, firearms and deer welfare.

4.12   Where possible, any person likely to be in the vicinity of the operation should be notified and requested to keep clear of the area.

4.13   General precautions in the interest of public safety on the discharge of firearms include warning neighbouring occupiers, the police and shooting away from roads, houses, gardens and livestock.

Night shooting

Code of Practice for Shooting Deer at Night

Prepared and published by the Deer Commission for Scotland in pursuance of Section 37(5)(a) of the Deer (Scotland) Act, 1996.

Any person issued with a night shooting authorisation is obliged to comply with this Code of Practice. Failure to do so can result in an authorisation being withdrawn.

1. Introduction

    The Deer (Scotland) Act, 1996 restricts the shooting of deer at night to those people with written authorisation from the Deer Commission for Scotland. The statutory definition is the period between the expiration of the first hour after sunset and the commencement of the last hour before sunrise.

    The Commission may authorise an occupier of agricultural land or of woodland, or any person nominated in writing by such an occupier, to shoot at night, any species of deer for the purpose of crop protection if such a person is considered fit and competent. The Commission must also be satisfied that night shooting is necessary to prevent serious damage and that no other method of control which might reasonably be adopted, would be adequate. Authorisations are subject to such conditions as may be specified, including the precise area to be covered, and the Commission will determine the period of its validity.

    If requested by the owner of the land, an occupier is obliged to supply, as soon as practicable after being requested to do so by the owner, information as to the numbers of deer of each species killed under such authorisations within the period of 12 months immediately preceding the date of request.

Firearms safety, the humane dispatch and welfare of deer are paramount in the issue of night shooting Authorisations and must be the overriding considerations of operators.

2. Compliance with the following conditions is obligatory
Night shooting Authorisations issued by the Commission contain the following obligatory conditions and will only be valid if these conditions are adhered to:

(1)   The local police must always be informed prior to night shooting being carried out.

(2)   For the killing of RED, SIKA, RED/SIKA CROSSES AND FALLOW DEER, a rifle of a calibre capable of firing ammunition of not less than 8.42 grams (130 grains) soft-nosed bullets, with a muzzle velocity of not less than 746.76 metres (2450 feet) per second *and* a muzzle energy of not less than 3051 joules (2250 foot/pounds) must be used.

(3)   For the killing of ROE DEER a rifle of a calibre capable of firing ammunition of not less than 6.48 grams (100 grains) soft-nosed bullets, with a muzzle velocity of not less than 746.76 metres (2450 feet) per second *and* a muzzle energy of not less than 2373 joules (1750 foot/pounds), must be used.

(4)   Where the use of a shotgun is authorised by the Deer Commission the bore and type of ammunition to be used will be specified in the Authorisation.

(5)   Authorisations must be returned to the Commission within 7 days of the date of expiry and include all details of the number and sex of deer killed.

3. Recommended operating team and equipment
For health and safety and animal welfare reasons the Commission recommends a minimum number of 2 operators when shooting at night.

However, the ideal crew for night operators should be: driver, light-operator and marksman. The duties of each person are:

Driver	To position the vehicle on instructions of the light-operator and to confirm the location of fallen animals.
Light-operator	To locate and select the most suitable targets and keep count of kills.
Marksman	To discharge the shot.

Whilst two people can operate successfully, a third makes the operation safer and more efficient. Where a vehicle is not used, an independent light-operator is essential.

Telescopic Sights	Should be not less than 4 × 36. The use of light-intensifying, heat sensitive or other special sighting devices is prohibited under section 5 of The Deer (Firearms etc.) (Scotland) Order, 1985.
Binoculars	7 or 8 × 50.
Spotlights	Operated from the vehicle battery, should be at least 250,000 candle power.
Hand-lights	12 volt 55 watt halogen bulb operated from a rechargeable power pack. Hand torches for carcase recovery are helpful.
Dogs	The use of a trained dog for carcase recovery is recommended, particularly in woodland.

4. Guidance and good practice

Before night shooting takes place operators must make themselves thoroughly familiar with the location where shooting is to be carried out and, where possible, neighbouring occupiers should be informed. Shooting should only be carried out in areas where there are suitable backstops. Particular attention must be paid to human habitation, roads, railways, footpaths and livestock.

Deer must be fully visible and clear of obstructions such as tree branches or foliage before a shot is attempted. The recommended distance is under 100 metres and the target area is the shoulder. Head or neck shots should not be attempted.

The provisions of section 20(1)(a) of the Deer (Scotland) Act, 1996 make it illegal to shoot deer from a moving vehicle. A vehicle bonnet or a roof hatch can, however, provide a platform for marksmen to gain accurate shots. Modern swivel type bipods can be advantageous. Shots should never be taken by stretching across the driver or passenger or across the roof of a vehicle because of the risk of someone emerging from the opposite door or simply walking unseen in front of the rifle. The use of an externally mounted shooting rail can enhance the efficiency of night shooting. Communication between the marksman and cab crew is essential and no person should step outside the vehicle unless given the all clear by the marksman.

In circumstances where it is unsafe to discharge a high velocity rifle, the Commission may authorise the use of a shotgun but will stipulate the bore and type of ammunition to be used.

All normal safety precautions relating to the use of firearms must be strictly observed.

Spotlighting is particularly effective for dealing with small groups of deer. Larger groups should be avoided as survivors may quickly associate danger with a bright light.

A first aid kit should always be carried and portable communication equipment is recommended. Details of location and expected time of return should be given to a third party.

CHAPTER 4

Crop Protection

Whilst deer stalking is important economically and socially, the regulation of deer numbers is now considered essential for many environmental reasons, including successful forestry and the welfare of the deer themselves. There will always be potential conflict where deer encroach on cultivated lands and need to be culled to protect crops.

Whilst the law can be an ass at times the legislators often have good reason for prohibiting certain activities, especially when they involve firearms with the potential for either a risk to public safety or unnecessary suffering to animals – the use of shotguns against deer, particularly roe, was once commonplace in some areas.

The economic implications of an expanding roe deer population was not realised in the early days – there was little protection for newly planted trees and deer-control policies were in their infancy. Deer management was often very crude. Roe were treated as vermin, just like the fox, and were dealt with in a similar manner, being driven to waiting guns and indiscriminately shot, often with shotguns. On many estates the fox and deer drives kept the roe in check, but the dreadful statistics told their own stories: a 20 per cent rate of kills to cartridges was considered above average. As a consequence many deer were left to die a painfully slow death. A few stalkers and deer managers, knowing the value of humane and selective culling, did much to educate those responsible to the more professional use of the rifle.

The change was incorporated into the legislation which now governs the choice of weapon to shoot deer: in England and Wales Schedule 2 of the Deer Act, 1991; in Northern Ireland the Wildlife (Northern Ireland) Order, 1985; and in Scotland the Deer (Firearms etc.) (Scotland) Order, 1985. The fundamental difference is that in England, Wales and Northern Ireland it is the calibre of the rifle that is the main criterion, while in Scotland it is the ammunition only – it is lawful to use any rifle capable of firing such ammunition. This is why the 22 centrefire, provided the energy requirements are met, is permitted against roe in Scotland but not in England.[51]

This situation is not ideal, especially for the stalker operating on both sides of the border. The spread of the diminutive muntjac could prompt changes to calibres, enabling the 22 centrefire to be used in England for the smaller species – it seems absurd that stalkers are restricted to using a calibre suitable for red and fallow on muntjac.

ENGLAND AND WALES

The Deer Act, 1991, provides for the taking of deer in certain situations during the close season for the purposes of crop protection. It also allows for the conditional use of shotguns at any time.

Section 7(1) allows an authorised person (see below) to shoot deer out of season on cultivated land, pasture or enclosed woodland provided that the conditions in section 7(3) apply. These are:

(a)   Deer of the same species are causing or had caused damage to crops, vegetables, fruit, growing timber or any other form of property on the land;
(b)   It is likely that further serious damage would be caused; and
(c)   Action was necessary to prevent it.

Although the Act does not define the meaning of crops, the scope appears to be very wide. This exception specifies crops, fruit and vegetables, but it may be possible to justify a case to include pasture especially when used for grazing. The term 'growing timber' implies any form of woodland or forestry, be it wild, managed or commercial. Areas of waste land or set-aside are unlikely to be classed as crops

51. See chapter 6 for more on firearms.

but it could be argued that they come under the term 'or any other form of property on the land'.

In most circumstances it is expected that a rifle meeting the requirements for deer control would be used. However there are further exceptions for authorised persons to use smooth-bore guns (shotguns) at any time of year.

Under section 7(2) an authorised person can also control any deer, on any land, at any time with a shotgun which is not less than a 12-bore and is loaded with either AAA shot or a single non-spherical bullet, not less than 350 grains (i.e. a rifled slug). A Firearm Certificate is required for the slug ammunition but not AAA. The authorised person must be able to show that the conditions under section 7(3) above apply.

An authorised person is:

(a)   the occupier of land on which the action is taken;
(b)   a resident member of the occupier's household authorised in writing by the occupier;
(c)   a person in the occupier's service [e.g. an employee] authorised in writing by the occupier; or
(d)   a person having the right to take or kill the deer on the land on which the action is taken or any person acting with the written authority of a person having that right [e.g. the shooting tenant or person authorised by him].

Where an authorised person takes action against marauding deer to protect his crops etc., the killing must take place on the land where the damage is occurring, not the land where the deer come from.

In the case of Traill v. Buckingham 1972, damage was being caused to crops on Buckingham's land. It was believed that the deer responsible were to be found in a wood adjoining his, but occupied by Traill. The wood had previously belonged to Buckingham's father, who sold it but retained the right to shoot deer and other animals in the wood. During the close season Buckingham entered the wood and shot a red hind. Although found not guilty of killing out of season at the magistrate's court, the Queen's Bench Division decided otherwise, on the basis that although he had the shooting rights in the wood, under the Deer Act, 1963, he was only entitled to deal with marauding deer on land where the damage was caused and not on adjoining land.

In this case the retention of shooting rights in the contract by Buckingham did not make him an occupier of his neighbour's wood or a person with the written authority of the occupier, who would be entitled to kill deer in the wood causing damage to the trees.

Sale of venison out of season

In the open seasons the occupier or stalker can only sell venison to a licensed game dealer. In the close seasons only a licensed game dealer can sell venison at all. The deer manager protecting crops who shoots more than he can eat or give away should therefore consider becoming a licensed game dealer. In this way sales can continue to a licensed dealer during the close season. Records of sales would, however, be required.[52]

SCOTLAND

The situation in Scotland is significantly different. The Deer Commission is empowered by the Deer (Scotland) Act, 1996, to advise landowners and occupiers on the conservation of land and the natural heritage. In severe cases the Deer Commission can require action to be taken and employ its own staff to carry out control measures.[53]

Under the Deer (Scotland) Act, 1996, it is lawful for a person to take or kill, and sell or dispose of, any deer found on:

1. arable land, improved permanent pasture (other than moorland) and land which has been regenerated so as to be able to make a significant contribution to the productivity of a holding which forms part of that agricultural land; or
2. enclosed woodland

where the occupier has reasonable ground for believing that serious damage will be caused to crops, pasture or human or animal food-stuffs on that agricultural land, or to that woodland, if the deer are not killed.

The action can be taken by the occupier or the following, authorised in writing by the occupier:

- the owner in person
- the owner's employees
- the occupier's employees
- any person normally resident on the land
- any other competent person approved in writing by the Deer Commission

52. See chapter 5.
53. See chapter 3.

As we saw in chapter 3, it is conceivable that a particular nominee might be competent to kill deer on the occupier's land if he lawfully held the required firearm for the purpose, but he might be considered unfit or unsuitable for the purpose by the Commission – for example, a notorious poacher or offender or someone who had otherwise come to adverse notice.

Woodland in this context means not just commercial forestry plantations but any land on which trees are grown, any such trees and also the vegetation amongst the trees on that land. A woodland is enclosed if it is surrounded by stock-proof, but not necessarily deer-proof, fencing or other barriers.

Serious damage is not defined and is a difficult area. It can be qualified in turnip fields, developing corn fields and silage fields but damage to permanent grassland is more difficult to assess. Damage to woodlands at different stages of woodland growth is quantifiable, e.g. browsing of leading shoots and bark stripping. Along with Scottish Natural Heritage the Commission is investigating methods for assessing damage to habitats and the significance of damage. In some communities browsing is beneficial in allowing species diversity.

Nothing contained in an agreement between an occupier and the owner of the land shall prohibit the above lawfully conducted control. However if the landowner or owner of the sporting rights believes that no damage is occurring or likely to occur they can challenge the actions or intentions of the tenant in court (section 26(3)).

Deer may be taken during the close season for reasons other than crop damage but only if such activities are authorised in writing by the Commission.

The Act does not cater for the use of shotguns but the Deer (Firearms etc.) Order, 1985, permits the persons listed above to use specified shotguns and ammunition for crop control as stated above. The shotgun must be not less than 12 gauge loaded with:

- for shooting any deer, a single rifled non-spherical slug not less than 380 grains or a cartridge loaded with SSG or larger
- for roe deer, a cartridge loaded with AAA or larger

Sale out of season

Unlike in England, there is no restriction on sale to a licensed dealer out of season provided the deer are lawfully killed.

NORTHERN IRELAND

Article 20(6) allows a person to kill or injure deer in the close season by shooting deer on cultivated land, enclosed pasture, enclosed woodland or garden grounds but that person must be able to satisfy a court:

(a) that he is an authorised person; and
(b) that he had reasonable grounds for believing that deer of the same species were causing, or had caused, serious damage to crops, pasture, vegetables, fruit, growing timber or any other form of property on that land, pasture, woodland or those grounds; and
(c) that there was likelihood of further damage and that such damage was likely to be serious; and
(d) that his action was necessary to prevent further damage.

An authorised person is:

- the occupier of the land on which the action is taken
- a resident member of his household authorised in writing by the occupier
- a person in his service (e.g. an employee) authorised in writing by the occupier
- any person having the right to take or kill the deer or a person authorised in writing by him (e.g. the shooting tenant, his gamekeeper and invited guns)

Under article 20(7), if deer are causing damage within the conditions specified in Article 20(6)(a) to (d) above an authorised person may use a smooth-bore gun to kill the deer on any such land, at any time, if it is not less than a 12-bore and is loaded with AAA shot or a single non-spherical bullet, not less than 22.68 grammes (350 grains), commonly known as a rifled slug.

Sale out of season

The requirements are the same as for England and Wales.

COMPENSATION

Domestic livestock are capable of trespass and it is possible to make a claim against the owner for the damage they cause under the Animals Act, 1971, or Animals (Scotland) Act, 1971. The position with wild animals is different, since they have no owner to make claims against.

Historically the tenant farmer on a sporting estate could only stand and watch as his master's quarry ravaged his crops. In 1880 the Ground Game Act eased the situation by granting tenants the right to take hares and rabbits – a right which could not be taken from or even signed away by the tenant in a contract.

The Deer (Scotland) Act, 1996, introduced a similar provision regarding deer. Under section 26(3) an occupier effectively has a concurrent right to take or kill deer for crop protection purposes in the circumstances described earlier. The section states that nothing contained in any agreement between an occupier of agricultural land (not moorland) or enclosed woodland and the owner shall prohibit the occupier from taking or killing deer to prevent serious crop damage. This provision would not prevent the occupier from also claiming compensation, but in practical terms it does give him lawful authority to protect his livelihood.

In England and Wales the law does not confer on the occupier the rights to take deer in this situation unless by agreement with the landowner or the person holding the sporting rights to the deer. In circumstances where the tenant of an agricultural holding suffers crop damage from deer and is restricted from culling them – i.e. the rights are vested in the owner or someone else and no written permission exists – a claim for compensation can be made under the Agricultural Holdings Act, 1986, or in Scotland the Agricultural Holdings (Scotland) Act, 1991.

To claim compensation, a tenant must give his landlord written notice within one month of the damage becoming evident and give him the opportunity to make an inspection of a growing crop before it is harvested or, if damaged after harvest, before it is removed from the land. A written notice of the claim is then sent to the landlord within one month after the expiry of the year in respect of which the claim is made. For the purposes of such a claim, a year normally ends on 29 September or another date agreed with the landlord. Where the shooting rights are held by a third person (e.g. a shooting tenant or syndicate), the landlord is entitled to be indemnified by the third party against such claims, which may be settled by arbitration under the Act.

RESTRICTION ON USE OF LEAD SHOT

The Environmental Protection (Restriction on Use of Lead Shot) (England) Regulations, 1999, made under section 140 of the

Environmental Protection Act, 1990 came into force on 1 September 1999 and currently apply to England only. It is anticipated that legislation will be introduced in Wales and Scotland in due course.

The Regulations seek to prevent the poisoning of wildfowl by ingestion of lead shot through feeding. Consequently the use of lead shot is now prohibited over land where waterfowl feed and over certain Sites of Special Scientific Interest (SSSIs) listed in the Regulations.

Although this will not impact on the use of a stalker's rifle (section firearms) it will apply to the use of shotguns where permitted for crop protection on any area where shot is likely to fall on or over the foreshore or any of the listed SSSIs.

Prohibition on use of cartridges containing lead shot

3. No person shall use lead shot for the purpose of shooting with a shot gun -

(a)   on or over any area below high-water mark of ordinary spring tides;

(b)   on or over any site of Special Scientific Interest included in Schedule 1 to these Regulations; or

(c)   any wild bird included in Schedule 2 to these Regulations i.e. duck, geese, snipe, golden plover, coot, moorhen and swan.

The Regulations grant powers to police officers and other persons 'authorised' by the Secretary of State.

Several scenarios spring to mind:

- A police officer may investigate a case where a shotgun has been used under the exemption for crop protection. If the area in question is on or adjacent to the foreshore or a listed SSSI enquiries may be made in respect of the type of shot used
- A police officer inspecting a game dealer's premises might come across deer carcases containing shot and ask questions about the shooter
- A warrant could be obtained to enter and examine premises if access is refused, for example an estate larder. An investigation could be quite wide and extend, for example to the examination of purchase records

CHAPTER 5

Dealing in Venison

This chapter covers the requirements of the Deer Acts as far as they relate to the sale of venison. It does not address additional food safety and hygiene legislation relating to processing establishments.

In recent years there has been a significant growth in U.K. super-market sales of game meat, and their overriding concerns are hygiene, traceability, animal welfare and consumer confidence. Supermarkets are increasingly managing the production from estate to store, including feed and use of drugs, to ensure traceability and quality. Such control is difficult with wild game and venison but supermar-kets do insist on certain standards in the processing of game once it reaches the licensed game dealer. The National Game Dealers Association (N.G.D.A.) is keen to portray venison as a high-quality product, but it is concerned about the threats to consumer and market confidence posed by poached deer. The sale or purchase of poached deer is a criminal offence.

Accurate dealer records and local-authority health inspections are seen as the way ahead, but the support of N.G.D.A. members, the police and the courts is vital. The B.A.S.C. campaign against poaching continues to raise awareness of the cruelty, hygiene and commercial issues involved with deer poaching and theft.

Licensed dealers are required to keep records that should identify the seller of a deer carcase. Accurate records ensure traceability and should identify poachers and their venison. In practice records are often incomplete through ignorance or intention and have received little police or local-authority attention in the past – but this may change.

In Devon the police have taken a proactive approach by sending a letter to every dealer explaining the record-keeping requirements of the Deer Act, which will then be subject to police inspection. Some dealers also voluntarily record details of firearm certificates. This is a good example of the police working in partnership with an industry that needs to respond by setting its records straight.

TAGGING

In 1996 the Scottish Office issued a consultation document on tagging schemes for wild deer carcases from Scotland. The main thrust of any tagging scheme would be to promote traceability and the quality of the product, which would subsequently benefit the industry through public confidence. For this reason the costs of a voluntary or compulsory scheme would have to be met by the industry – generally the government is seeking to deregulate where appropriate and would need to be convinced that the advantages of compulsory tagging would outweigh the burdens it will impose.

Traditionally tagging has been seen as a means to control poaching.

There seems little doubt that a rigorous system of carcase identification would help to identify illegally killed deer and consequently tackle this activity more effectively. However, existing legislation does provide numerous offences and extensive powers for the police and prosecution authorities. The problem here is one of enforcement, and the government would need to be convinced that tagging as an anti-poaching measure would be substantially more effective than existing controls.

The documents raised several other issues regarding enforcement, cross-border sales, the collection of data on deer culls, the cost of tags and administration.

Forest Enterprise has established its own voluntary scheme. As the agency managing the Forestry Commission's estate, it is the largest single supplier of wild deer carcases in the country. In the 1980s the North Scotland Region introduced a system of tagging for all carcases. Forest Enterprise sees the tagging system as having the following key benefits:

- It allows traceability of carcases back to the ranger responsible for shooting and preparation, which has led to an increase in standards of venison handling
- It guarantees association of carcase and pluck when the carcases are inspected at game dealers by a vet
- It ensures that the property of Forest Enterprise is securely identifiable and cannot be switched with other carcases, either accidentally or intentionally
- It provides a secure basis for collection information about deer shot to be used to manage deer populations objectively

The system used by North Scotland Region has now been extended to other Forest Enterprise regions including England and Wales.

Under French law deer hunting is subject to annual 'hunting plans', normally organised at departmental (county) level, which set out the number of animals of the different species that can be shot during the season. People with the right to hunt can only hunt deer if they are granted by the authority responsible for the hunting plan an individual allocation of deer they can kill. Control of the exercise of individual allocations is carried out by the issue of tags, for a fee, which are attached to the individual carcases when killed. At the end of each hunting season individuals in receipt of tags have to account for their use to the authorities and to return unused tags. Failure to comply with the requirements is subject to penalties. This tagging is seen as an environmental and anti-poaching measure, however, and does not play a role in meat hygiene controls.

Similarly in Germany, deer hunting is strictly controlled by the relevant authorities at the local level, largely with the aim of conserving stocks at sustainable levels. Those who wish to hunt deer need to apply to the authorities every year for an allocation of animals they can hunt. A federal law requiring the compulsory tagging of wild deer carcases (as an anti-poaching measure) was repealed in the mid-1970s but compulsory tagging was recently reintroduced in Brandenburg, where poaching is considered a major problem.

In July 1998 the N.G.D.A. launched its own voluntary tagging scheme for processors, which promised to improve the traceability of carcases. Developed by the Scottish arm of the N.G.D.A. and with

69

input from the Association of Deer Management Groups and the British Deer Society, only members who are veterinary inspecting carcases are eligible to join the scheme and use the two-part official tags for carcase and pluck.

The scheme's aim is to provide traceability for health and safety reasons, to provide consumer confidence in the finished product and to help eliminate the substantial black market in venison carcases which serves to undermine market stability and consumer confidence. Initially the scheme is to run as a pilot in Scotland, with a view to rolling it out in England and Wales at a later date. Members buy strips of the official tags from the N.G.D.A. and then give their estates the two-part tags to use on all their carcases. They will then only accept for processing carcases which carry the official tags.

An N.G.D.A. spokesman said at the launch, 'The scheme is reliant on members' integrity to work well, but we hope it will help improve a difficult market, and demonstrate to legislators that the game processing industry is working hard to put its own house in order. The scheme will also complement ASSURED BRITISH GAME as it applies to wild venison. If processors and estates are to develop a competitive home market for wild venison, they must become more customer focused. Carcase tagging is just one part of this progression.'

CONTROLS ON VENISON DEALING

Several laws apply to game dealing and processing, starting with the Game Act, 1831. The Game Act, 1970, introduced some amendments but the legislation does not cater for today's society or markets, a situation which may be resolved by a government review which is underway.

The Game Act, 1831, requires dealers in game to be licensed in England. Game means game birds and hares. Section 13 of the Game Licences Act, 1860, extends the provisions to Wales and Scotland. Northern Ireland is covered by the Game Preservation Act (Northern Ireland), 1928, the Wildlife (Northern Ireland) Order, 1985, and the Miscellaneous Transferred Excise Duties Act (Northern Ireland), 1972. There are several loopholes in respect of game but the subsequent deer legislation has included amendments on venison dealing which make the situation clearer.

In England, Wales and Northern Ireland the sale of venison to the public is restricted to licensed game dealers only. In Scotland licensed game dealers may only trade in game and persons wishing to trade in venison are subject to an additional licensing procedure under the

Deer (Scotland) Act, 1996. Transactions may be made between English and Scottish dealers, provided that they are recorded on the prescribed forms and that both parties are licensed in their own countries. There is no such restriction on the importation of venison from other countries other than that details of the transaction would need to be recorded. In Northern Ireland there is also no restriction on lawfully imported venison other than recording the transactions.

Generally the Deer Acts apply to farmed deer only in certain circumstances, for example killing out of season, method of killing and sale of carcases, and such matters are covered in chapters 2 and 3. Sales of live deer are not governed by the Acts but carcases and venison from any source, wild or farm, are subject to controls.

England and Wales

In England and Wales the issue of a game dealer's licence is mostly a formality. First an applicant registers the business with the local authority. The registration is often recorded by the Environmental Health Department and enables inspection of premises for public health purposes. There is no central register of dealers or premises and enquiries to identify all dealers in an area will require checks with each local authority district.

The second stage is to obtain an excise licence from the post office where it is a condition of issue that a local authority licence is produced. The excise licence expires on 1 July each year. The excise licence must be renewed but the local authority may not require renewal of their licence. For a few pounds anyone can set up a processing business with little control or inspection. At the other end of the scale are the major processors with hi-tech plants and veterinary inspections.

Export and import

There is no restriction on stalkers importing or exporting venison or wild boar within the European Union or to or from the United States. The situation is similar to that of cigarettes and alcohol – the stalker must satisfy H.M. Customs that it is for personal use or consumption. Large amounts, perhaps several carcases, may be considered to be commercial and attract attention from environmental health authorities. Trophies in the raw state are not restricted but mounted specimens may be subject to V.A.T.

More exotic species may be protected by the Convention on the International Trade in Endangered Species (CITES), which requires documentation at the point of export and import. Check before you travel.

Sale and purchase

The Deer Act, 1991, does not control the sale of live deer, only venison and carcases which are defined by section 16. Farmed venison is governed by the controls on sale. The term 'deer' means any species and includes the carcase or any part of it: 'venison' includes imported meat and means the carcase, or any edible part of the carcase, which has not been canned or cooked.

The reference to canned or cooked venison is similar to the exception in the Game Act which permits an innkeeper to sell game for consumption on his premises, but the Deer Act is far wider in its scope in that any person could sell cooked or canned venison which he had obtained lawfully. However a butcher or supermarket selling uncooked processed venison, such as venison sausages or chilled or frozen joints, would need to be licensed as a game dealer. Each shop would need to be licensed individually with the local authority.

Note that the definition and consequently the licensing requirements apply to all imported venison.

Section 10(1)(a) of the Deer Act, 1991, states that it is an offence for anyone other than a licensed game dealer to sell, offer or expose for sale or possess for sale any venison during the prohibited period. This period only relates to venison from a species protected by a close season (i.e. red, fallow, roe and sika) and begins ten days after the start of the relevant close season. Therefore a stalker may only sell, or possess for sale, such venison during the open season and the first ten days of the relevant close season. Licensed dealers may possess and sell during the prohibited period.

Under section 10(1)(b), it is an offence for anyone other than a licensed dealer to sell, offer or expose for sale venison at any time unless the sale is to a licensed dealer. In effect the stalker wishing to sell venison direct to friends or to a restaurant must be licensed as a dealer.

Section 10(3)(4) provides that it is also an offence for anyone to sell, possess for sale, purchase, offer to purchase or receive venison from any deer which he knows or believes has been illegally taken or killed under any preceding provisions of the Deer Act (close season or unlawful methods).

Licensed dealers should take care to ensure the origin of the carcases offered to them, as failure to do so may render them liable. Turning a blind eye to the following may prove expensive:

- failure to keep full and accurate records
- buying carcases with dog marks
- buying carcases with shotgun wounds

- buying carcases shot with unlawful weapons – especially .22 rimfire and crossbow
- buying out of season – a dealer ought to be able to sex a deer in carcase form and should be aware of the close season for the male and female of the species

Sale out of season

The Deer Act, 1991, exempts the killing of deer out of season by occupiers of land (to prevent crop damage) and deer farmers. But there is provision for deer legally killed out of season to be sold by the occupier, stalker or deer farmer to a licensed dealer. Section 10(1)(a) allows dealers to sell and possess venison during the close season, but doing so during the close season is an offence for non-dealers. An occupier who finds it necessary to cull deer in the close season must either consume the venison, preserve it until the open season or give it away. If he wishes to sell it he must become a licensed game dealer to remove the restriction imposed by section 10(1)(a). In effect he would be able to sell to his usual processor but must also comply with conditions in respect of displaying a dealer's sign on the premises, the keeping and inspection of records etc.

Sexing carcases

This is relatively straightforward if one is presented with the whole animal. However a headless and gralloched beast is more difficult and may require internal examination. In some cases the mere weight can be an indicator. The pelvic conformation is reliable in the skeleton but not in the hanging carcase, although the internal shape and size of the pelvic canal may give a guide. If the posterior abdominal muscles are intact (i.e. if the linea alba has simply been split without trimming muscle around the udder or scrotum) then the inguinal canals give a good guide, since the male will have cremaster muscle and probably remnants of the tunica vaginalis and cord through the ring, which is larger than in the female.

If this tissue has been trimmed, there are differences between the male and female blood vessels arising from the aorta, since the spermatic arteries are far smaller than the corresponding uterine arteries and the internal pudendal artery in the male is far larger than in the female.

However clean the carcase, it should always be possible to detect the sites of attachments of the broad ligament of the uterus and of the ovarian ligaments and finally, the root of the penis is usually left in place as it courses over the posterior rim of the pubis.

Records

Section 11 requires a licensed dealer to keep records in a book in the format shown in Schedule 3 to the Act or a form substantially the same.[54] The term 'book' and the need to ensure accuracy and traceability tends to preclude the use of loose sheets. The Act is silent on the use of computerised systems.

The dealer must enter, or cause to be entered, in his record book 'forthwith' full particulars of all his purchases and receipts of venison. 'Forthwith' is not defined in the Act but the dictionary says 'immediately, at once, right away' and as Schedule 3 requires such details as the identity of the seller and the registration number of the vehicle it seems appropriate to do so at the time.

Where venison is purchased or received from another dealer in England and Wales, or from a licensed venison dealer in Scotland, only the following details need to be recorded:

- that the venison was received
- the name and address of the other dealer
- the date purchased/received
- the total weight of the venison

For sales to a dealer in Scotland, additional details are also required by the Scottish dealer:

- the number of carcases and sex of the venison
- the species of deer, provided it is possible to identify it

All transactions relating to imported venison need to be fully documented as required by Schedule 3.

A council official authorised in writing or a police officer may inspect:

- the record book of a licensed dealer
- venison in the licensed dealer's possession or under his control
- venison on the premises, or in vehicles under his control
- any invoices and other documents which relate to the records

They may also take copies or extracts from the record book and documents.

The book must be retained for three years from the last entry and

54. See page 80.

other documents for three years from the date of the entry relating to them.

It is an offence to fail to comply with this section, to obstruct an official or police officer, or knowingly or recklessly to make or cause to be made a false or misleading entry in a record book.

Unlike Scotland, where a warrant may be obtained, there are no specific powers for police officers to enter and inspect the premises of unlicensed dealers, or the facility to obtain a warrant, but local authority environmental health officers have their own powers to inspect premises involved in food preparation.

On conviction for any offence under the Act, section 13 states that the court may order the forfeiture of any deer or venison found in the person's possession together with any vehicle, animal, weapon or other thing used to commit the offence. In addition, if the offence is under sections 1 (poaching), 10 (venison dealing) or 11 (dealers' records) the court may also disqualify the person from holding or obtaining a game dealer's licence for such period as the court thinks fit. The court may also cancel any firearm or shotgun certificate held by him.

Northern Ireland

A game dealer's licence is issued in Northern Ireland by the Department of Health and Social Services which administers the Miscellaneous Transferred Excise Duties Act (Northern Ireland), 1972. Applicants must first obtain a Certificate of Good Character from a Magistrate's Court. This legislation also extends the definition of game to include deer for game-dealing purposes.

The Game Preservation Act (Northern Ireland), 1928, sections 3 and 3A require dealers to keep a register of the prescribed form to be kept for three years, together with invoices and other documentation. This aspect is the responsibility of the Department of Environment. Hygiene is the responsibility of the Department of Agriculture.

The main offences relating to dealing in venison are found in the Wildlife (Northern Ireland) Order, 1985, but there are numerous other offences relating to game dealers in the Miscellaneous Transferred Excise Duties Act.

The term 'venison' includes imported meat and means the carcase, or any edible part of the carcase, but not canned or cooked venison.

Under Article 23(1), it is an offence for anyone other than a licensed game dealer to sell, offer or expose for sale or possess for sale any venison during the prohibited period. The prohibited period only relates to venison from a species protected by a close season (i.e. red, fallow, and sika), and begins ten days after the start of the relevant close season. Therefore a stalker may only sell, or possess for sale, such venison during the open season and the first ten days of the relevant close season. Licensed dealers may possess and sell during the prohibited period.

Article 23(1) states that it is an offence for anyone other than a licensed dealer to sell, offer or expose for sale venison at any time unless the sale is to a licensed dealer. A stalker wishing to sell venison direct to friends or to a restaurant must therefore be licensed as a dealer, even in the open season. Under Article 23(2), it is also an offence for anyone to sell, possess for sale, purchase, offer to purchase or receive venison from any deer which he knows or believes has been illegally taken or killed under the Order e.g. close season or unlawful methods.

Licensed dealers should take care to ensure the origin of the carcases offered to them as failure to do so may render them liable. In particular, they should beware of the following:

- failure to keep full and accurate records
- buying carcases with dog marks
- buying carcases with shotgun wounds
- buying carcases shot with unlawful weapons – especially .22 and crossbow
- buying out of season – a dealer ought to be able to sex a deer in carcase form and should be aware of the close season for male and female of the species[55]

Records
Section 3 and 3A of the Game Preservation Act (Northern Ireland) as amended by the Wildlife (Northern Ireland) Order require the keeping of records in a prescribed form.

Scotland

Most of the Deer (Scotland) Act, 1996, relates only to those species of deer defined in an Order made by the Secretary of State. But the sections of the Act controlling the sale of venison include all species and farmed venison. 'Venison' is defined by section 33(7) as the carcase or any edible part of the carcase of a deer, and 'deer' means deer of any species, whether or not deer within the meaning of section 45 of the Act, and includes farmed venison.

---

55. See page 73 on the sexing of carcases.

Anyone wishing to trade in wild or farmed venison is required to be licensed under the Deer (Scotland) Act, 1996. The main difference between England and Scotland is that licensed game dealers in England may deal in both game and venison, whereas in Scotland a quite separate licence is required for a venison dealer, who must first go through a vetting procedure. The Deer Commission also has a statutory role in the regulation and inspection of venison dealers, whereas such a body does not exist south of the border.

Under the Licensing of Venison Dealers (Application Procedures etc.) (Scotland) Order, 1984, licences in Scotland are granted by island or district councils and are valid for three years. The application can be made by an individual or by his agent involved in the day-to-day running of the business, perhaps the manager of one of his premises. Full names and addresses of the applicants are required. If the applicant is a company, details of the registered office, directors, partners, etc. are also needed. In both cases, the address of any premises used for handling the venison within the area of the authority must be included, together with any other information which may be additionally required by the authority.

Copies of an application for the grant or renewal of a licence are sent to the local chief constable and fire authority, and to the Deer Commission. The authority may then make enquiries as to the suitability of the applicant and may take the results into account when considering the application; but where they intend to do so, the applicant must be notified and given the opportunity to reply.

The authority may refuse an application, but must give reasons for doing so. If a licence is granted or renewed, it may be subject to reasonable conditions, which may include the inspection of venison. Where a licence is not granted or renewed, the applicant may lodge an appeal to the sheriff within twenty-eight days.

A person dealing only in venison does not require an excise licence. Issuing councils must supply details of licence holders to the Deer Commission, chief constable and fire authority.

Records
Section 34 of the Act requires the keeping of records and the Licensing of Venison Dealers (Prescribed Forms etc.) (Scotland) Order, 1984, prescribes the format of records to be kept[56] which must be in a book. This appears to prohibit the use of loose sheets which may be altered and replaced, but the Deer Commission accepts computerised systems. As in England and Wales, the dealer must

---

56. See page 81.

enter in his record book forthwith full particulars of all his purchases and receipts of venison.

Where venison is purchased or received from another dealer, or from a licensed game dealer in England, the following details need to be recorded:

- that the venison was received
- the name and address of the other dealer
- the date purchased/received
- the species of deer, provided it is possible to identify it
- the number of carcases and sex of the venison[57]

All imports of venison from other countries need to be fully documented.

A police officer or a person authorised in writing by the Secretary of State or the Deer Commission may inspect the records. The dealer shall produce for inspection:

- the record book
- any invoices and other documents which relate to the records
- all venison in his possession or under his control
- venison on premises, or in vehicles under his control

He must also allow copies or extracts from the record book or documents to be made.

The book must be retained for three years from the last entry and other documents for three years from the date of the entry relating to them.

Offences

Section 36 contains a number of offences in relation to venison dealing.

Under section 36(1), it is an offence for someone to sell, offer for sale, possess or transport for the purpose of sale at any premises, any venison unless

1. he is a licensed venison dealer; or
2. he is in possession or transporting for the purpose of selling to such a dealer; [e.g. a stalker or landowner] or
3. he has purchased the venison from a licensed dealer [e.g. a butcher].

---

57. see page 73 on sexing of carcases.

A police officer may obtain a search warrant to enter unlicensed premises.

Unlike in English legislation, canned and cooked venison come within the Scottish definition, but section 3 permits the hotelier to serve venison if it is purchased from a venison dealer. Indeed, it would appear that any unlicensed person – a butcher or supermarket, for example – may sell or possess venison if purchased from a licensed venison dealer. Frozen and processed venison purchased from a licensed dealer can also be sold in unlicensed shops. Moreover, in contrast to the situation in England and Wales, in Scotland the transaction is not related to a prohibited period, the only provision being that the deer was lawfully killed.

Under section 36(4), it is an offence to sell, offer for sale, possess for sale, transport for sale, purchase or receive any carcase which one knows or has reason to believe was unlawfully killed. Licensed dealers should in fact take care to ensure they know the origin of the carcases offered to them as failure to do so may render them liable. Turning a blind eye to the following may prove expensive:

- failure to keep full and accurate records
- buying carcases with dog marks
- buying carcases with shotgun wound
- buying carcases shot with unlawful weapons – especially .22 rimfire and crossbow
- buying out of season – a dealer ought to be able to sex a deer in carcase form and should be aware of the close season for male and female of the species.[58]

Any licensed venison dealer who fails to keep records or makes false entries commits an offence (section 36(5)), as does anyone obstructing the inspection of such records (section 36(6)). Section 34(5) provides that anyone convicted of an offence under Part III of the Act (illegal taking of deer) or section 36 (venison dealing offences) may be disqualified by the court from holding or obtaining a venison dealer's licence.

---

58. See page 73 on the sexing of carcases.

PRESCRIBED RECORD FORMS

England and Wales

Section 11.

SCHEDULE 3

Form of Record to be kept by Licensed Game Dealers

Date of purchase or receipt*	Species	Means by which the deer was killed†	Particulars of carcases purchased or received					Particulars of parts of carcases purchased or received			Particulars of seller, or in the case of a receipt the source‡ from which receipt obtained, and registration number of vehicle delivering venison
			Male		Female		Total	Number (of parts)	Description (of parts)	Weight	
			No.	Weight	No.	Weight	No.	Weight				

* Where the venison comes from deer killed by the dealer, enter date of killing.
† If killed by rifle or smooth-bore gun, enter "rifle" or "smooth-bore gun".
‡ Where the venison comes from deer killed by the dealer, enter name of premises or place in which killed.

Scotland

SCHEDULE

FORM OF RECORDS OF PURCHASES AND RECEIPTS OF VENISON TO BE KEPT BY LICENSED VENISON DEALERS

Date of purchase or receipt*	Species	Place where deer killed, eg name of estate, agricultural holding, or forest	Name and address of seller, or in the case of receipt the source from which the venison was received[x]	Registration number of vehicle delivering venison	Particulars of carcases purchased or received						Particulars of parts of carcases purchased or received		
					Male		Female		Total		Number (or parts)	Description (or parts)	Weight
					No.	Weight	No.	Weight	No.	Weight			

*Where the venison comes from deer killed by the dealer (including his employee or agent), enter date of killing.
[x]Where the venison comes from deer killed by the dealer (including his employee or agent), enter 'killed by dealer'.

HYGIENE AND THE HANDLING OF VENISON

The following is reproduced from the manual *Guidance on Recommended Standards for Wild Game* produced by the Local Authorities Co-ordinating Body on Food and Trading Standards (LACOTS). We are indebted to John Adams, a LACOTS adviser on wild game, for his assistance.

The manual examines minimum standards and good practice for those parts of the domestic U.K. game industry which are subject to the Food Safety (General Food Hygiene) Regulations, 1995 and equivalent legislation in Northern Ireland.

The guidelines do not provide advice on the Wild Game Meat (Hygiene and Inspection) Regulations, 1995, which apply to premises producing wild game meat to E.U. standards, i.e. for export to other member states or for supply to customers in Great Britain who require the health mark.

The National Game Dealers' Association supports the guidance, which it promotes to members.

Personal hygiene for stalkers

- to prevent the contamination of venison
- to prevent personal infection

These basic objectives can be achieved by rangers/stalkers observing strict personal hygiene standards when working or visiting larders and when transporting deer carcases and organs.

The following are some basic hygiene rules:

- boots must be washed and disinfected before entering a larder
- wear protective clothing when working or visiting larders or handling deer carcases

- wash hands immediately before and after using the toilet
- keep cuts and sores covered with a waterproof dressing
- do not smoke in larders
- report diarrhoea, nausea or sickness or any infection likely to cause food poisoning to senior management and the local authority environmental health department
- boots must be washed and disinfected before leaving the larder

Protective clothing

The purpose of protective clothing is to prevent the contamination of venison by bacteria from personal clothing. Positive and effective management will ensure that no person enters a larder without suitable protective clothing. This rule must also apply to any visitor to a larder since they may bring in bacteria from other sources. The minimum requirements are a washable white overall or long coat, protective industrial footwear and white safety hat with a net for longer hair, and a white waterproof apron and leggings and plastic gloves.

Clean overalls or coats must be issued daily. Waterproof items must be cleansed at regular intervals throughout the working day.

Personal cleanliness

It is essential that all rangers/stalkers pay particular importance to personal cleanliness. The objective is not only to prevent contamination of venison but also to protect themselves from infection. Hands must be washed at regular intervals when handling venison, particularly after handling diseased or contaminated carcases. Rangers/stalkers should seek treatment for every wound, no matter how slight.

General note

Management must ensure that all rangers/stalkers are aware that their personal habits may lead to contamination of venison. They should not be allowed to cull and process deer until they have been instructed about possible dangers of infection to venison and themselves. Handwashing is the most effective means of avoiding the transfer of bacteria from the person and should be undertaken at regular intervals during the handling of venison.

Annex 1: Advisory notes on dressing and inspection technique

Information for use by local authority inspectors and proprietors/estate managers
Game culled for human consumption must be handled correctly and hygienically, from the point where it is shot through to the point of sale to the final consumer.

Dressing and inspection of deer carcases
The most practical and hygienic environment for dressing carcases is in a properly constructed larder. However, with wild deer, this is not always possible because some of the larger species of deer need to be physically dragged or carried back from remote and inaccessible places to the larder by the hunter. In these circumstances, to reduce the weight of the carcase, the deer has to be gralloched (eviscerated) where it is shot, and the stomach, intestines and mesenteric lymph nodes will need to be examined for disease by the hunter before they are disposed of. During hunting of the live animal and subsequent gralloching or removal of the head, the hunter may come across abnormalities. These should be recorded and notified to the game-processing establishment, either directly or via the operator of the collecting centre.

Dressing/tagging procedures
The following are recommended dressing procedures that should be undertaken when culling wild deer for human consumption:

- Deer in the wild are shot either in the neck or chest.
- After the animal has been shot, it must be immediately bled by cutting the main vessels and arteries in the neck. At this point, the oesophagus should be tied to avoid stomach contents contaminating the carcase.
- Free anus by cutting in a full circle

When field dressing, there are two methods used for gralloching:

(a) suspended dressing – the carcase should be opened cleanly with a cut from aitches to brisket
(b) ground dressing – open carcase with a cut from brisket to aitches

Whether field or larder dressing, care should be taken not to puncture bladder, stomach or intestines.

Stomach and intestines should be removed cleanly. Examine and, if necessary, incise mesenteric lymph nodes. When field dressing, ensure stomach and intestines are disposed of safely to avoid passing on possible diseases or parasites to other animals.

The heart, lungs, liver, kidneys, spleen and, where practical, head should remain with or be otherwise identifiable to the carcase. If removed it is suggested that they should remain identifiable with the carcase by using a system of tamperproof tags. This is to ensure that the organs (and the head) can be identified with the carcase up to the time of inspection by the processor. Note that whilst some hunters remove heads for trophies, others retain jawbones for ageing. If the head is removed for these purposes it should be inspected by the ranger/stalker (who should keep records of abnormalities with tag references and notify these to the processor). Irrespective of whether the head or organs are removed, it is recommended that carcases are tagged where necessary to enable venison processors/dealers to trace the originating ranger/stalker.

Inspection of deer carcase and organs
The following are recommended post-mortem inspection procedures for determining the fitness of wild deer.

General instructions
The carcase, organs and blood of culled deer must be examined without undue delay. Regard must be given to:

- The age and sex of the deer.
- The state of nutrition of the deer.
- Any evidence of bruising or haemorrhage.
- Any indications of faecal contamination or decomposition. Any local or general oedema.
- The efficiency of bleeding.
- Any swelling, deformity or other abnormality of bones, joints or musculature. Any abnormality in consistency or colour.
- The condition of the pleura and peritoneum.
- Signs indicating the presence of veterinary drug residues or poisoning from environmental contamination or pesticides.
- An animal suspected of being diseased must be rejected or detained for further detailed post-mortem examination by a qualified person. An arrangement could be made with the local authority for an Environmental Health Officer or Authorised Meat Inspector to call on request.
- The possibility of death due to anthrax infection must not be overlooked in the case of moribund/sick deer or dead animals found in the wild.

- Any injured animal should be detained for detailed post-mortem examination by a qualified person.
- Deer that have died as a result of a road accident or found dead from some other cause must never be processed for human consumption.

Post mortem inspection

HEAD
- Examine lips and tongue (Disease: Foot and Mouth Disease).
- Examine jaw bones (Disease: Actinomycosis).
- Examine and incise retropharyngeal and submaxillary lymph nodes (Disease: Tuberculosis, Abscesses and Actinobacillosis).
- Examine stomach and intestines.
- Examine and incise mesenteric lymph nodes (Disease: Tuberculosis, Enteritis, Abscesses; Cysticercus Tenuicollis and Tumours).

SPLEEN
- Examine surface (Disease: if enlarged, suspect Anthrax).

LIVER
- Examine surface (Disease: if enlarged, suspect Anthrax).
- Examine portal lymph nodes and, if considered necessary, incise. Examine surface and substance and, if necessary, incise (Diseases: Liver Fluke, Tuberculosis, Hepatitis, Cysticercus Tenuicollis, Hydatid Cyst, fatty change, Tumours and Abscesses).

LUNGS
- Examine and, if necessary, incise right and left bronchial lymph nodes.
- Examine and, if necessary, incise mediastinal lymph nodes.
- Examine and palpate lungs and, if necessary, incise (Diseases: Pneumonial, Pleurisy, Tuberculosis, Hydatid Cysts, Lung Worms, Tumours and Abscesses).

HEART
- Open pericardium and examine heart muscle. If necessary, incise and examine substance and internal surfaces (Diseases: Pericarditis, Septic-pericarditis and Cysts).

KIDNEYS
- Expose and examine external surface and, if necessary, incise (Diseases: Hydronephrosis, Nephritis and Cysts).

CARCASE
- Examine internal and external surfaces, also joints (Diseases: Arthritis, Abscesses, Tuberculosis, Bruising (extensive and severe), Oedema, Pyrexia, emaciation (pathological) and Uraemia).

Annex 2: Standards for wild game larders/collection centres

The term used in these guidelines 'larders/collection centres' means: any premises or place where killed wild game is kept prior to being transported for further preparation at a wild game processing establishment. The terms 'larder', 'game larder' and 'collection centre' are interchangeable but whatever term is used the Food Safety (General Food Hygiene) Regulations, 1995, will apply (even if some or all of the stored meat may be subsequently transported to an EC approved processing establishment).

The primary functions of a larder/collection centre are:

- Initial cooling of carcases.
- Providing temporary storage to hang wild game carcases under hygienic, vermin and fly-proof conditions prior to despatch to a game processing establishment

These guidelines are applicable only where handling is limited to the storage of unskinned or feathered carcases, or to the removal of feet, heads and green/red offal of deer carcases or other large wild game animals. It is implicit that larders/collection centres are used solely for the short term storage of wild game, pending collection and consignment to game processing premises or similar establishments.

General note

Furred and feathered game should be separated, each having its own hanging area to prevent cross-contamination. The rooms should have a high ceiling to allow the heat to disperse over the hanging game, together with the provision of adequate fly-proof air vents at ceiling and floor level to create a cooling air flow.

Wild game carcases should be hung with adequate separation from each other to allow good air circulation for rapid cooling. When siting new collection centres shady areas or north-facing slopes should be chosen where possible to minimise the heating effect of the sun especially during the summer. Best practice, wherever practicable, would be to provide a refrigerated chill room.

If tagging of large wild game carcases has not been done previously by the hunter (see Annex 1), it is suggested that this should be done at the collection centre even if the pluck/head are not removed. (The tagging of carcases will help venison dealers comply with their licensing obligations to keep records as to the origin of the meat for traceability purposes).

Ventilation

The principal factor contributing to the successful storage of wild game is ventilation. Wild game carcases will rapidly go mouldy under damp conditions. Windows, doors and air vents must be fly-screened and bird- and rodent-proofed.

Floors and walls

An impervious, non-slip floor must be provided.

Walls must be smooth and impervious, capable of being readily cleaned. Both walls and floors should be proofed against pests.

Wash-hand facilities

Facilities must be provided for the hygienic washing and drying of hands. Ideally this should be a wash-hand basin provided with hot and cold water or suitably controlled heated water and materials for cleaning hands and hygienic drying. In remote locations portable facilities may be used.

Sink/Wash-hand basin

A sink supplied with cold and where practicable hot water should be provided. In small one-man-operation larders where very little or no dressing takes place the provision of a combined wash-hand basin and sink is acceptable.

Water supply/standpipe

There must be an adequate supply of ideally mains water. Any water in contact with foodstuffs or used for cleaning work tools and equipment in contact with food must be potable. Consideration should be given to the provision of a standpipe and hose to facilitate washing down the larder when empty.

Lighting

Where necessary, adequate artificial lighting should be provided. Such lighting should provide not less than 220 lux. In remote parts of the country where there is no supply of electricity, larders/collection centres should be designed to provide maximum natural illumination of the premises.

Effluent

The drainage should preferably be connected to the public sewage system. In the absence of mains sewage, the effluent should be linked to a septic tank. It is accepted that for small collection centres in particularly remote areas such arrangements may not be justified or practicable.

Work surfaces
All surfaces should be provided with a smooth, durable and impervious finish, capable of being readily cleaned.

Segregation of wild game
A wild game larder/collection centre should not be used for the storage of small or feathered game at the same time as eviscerated deer carcases, other than by the provision of a separate larder, or a designated area so designed to prevent cross-contamination.

Waste disposal
Suitable facilities should be provided for the hygienic storage of food waste arising from work undertaken in, or in connection with, the larder/collection centre. Receptacles provided for this purpose should be of impervious construction, fitted with close-fitting lids and stored away from food areas.

General hygiene
Larders/collection centres must be kept clean and in such a state of repair as to enable them to be effectively cleaned.

Note regarding meat destined for an EC Approved Establishment
For meat destined for an EC Approved Establishment it is envisaged that the carcase should arrive at the processing establishment within 12 hours of being killed unless chilling facilities are provided at the collection centre for chilling to a temperature not exceeding 7°C for large wild game and 4°C for small game. If such facilities are provided a further 12 hours is permissible before arrival at the processing establishment.

It is recognised, however, that in isolated rural areas particularly in Scotland these standards will not always be achievable. In such cases and where collection centres do not have refrigerated storage facilities, the storage of wild game is limited by climatic conditions and suitable precautions should be taken to ensure the wild game remains in a fit condition and is transported as quickly as possible to the processing establishment.

Annex 3: Hygiene and cleaning of larders and processing establishments

Principles of cleaning
It is essential that those involved with hygiene management should institute regular cleaning programmes, which must include both

equipment and premises. It is the responsibility of management to ensure that systematic daily cleaning takes place.

Effective cleaning must be part of normal larder operations and will need to include the regular use of appropriate detergents, disinfectants and possibly sanitisers.

General cleaning

Stalkers should be encouraged to keep the larders and equipment as clean as possible during the dressing of deer carcases. If stomachs and intestines are removed in the larder; after inspection they must be deposited in metal or plastic containers with closely fitting lids, such containers being disinfected daily.

In processing establishments parts removed from the carcase should be placed in specially provided containers or hung on stainless steel racks or hooks to await inspection. Offal and heads must not be placed on the floor.

Dropped waste scraps of meat, fat and blood must be removed and placed in impervious waste containers with closely fitting lids, which should be clearly marked 'NOT FIT FOR HUMAN CONSUMPTION'.

The primary objective of general cleaning is to keep gross contamination to a minimum, thus making later thorough cleaning an easier task.

Daily cleaning

The final daily cleaning programme should commence immediately after the premises are clear of carcases and offal. A thorough general cleaning followed by hosing down of floors, walls and equipment should be undertaken. Detergents and disinfectants must be used daily to ensure that there is no build-up of harmful bacteria within the larder. (Foaming agents can be effective for routine cleaning purposes.)

Weekly cleaning programme

A detailed weekly cleaning and disinfection programme must be undertaken. However, it must not cause daily routines to be neglected. The majority of detergent, disinfectant and foaming agent manufacturers will readily prepare systematic and thorough cleaning schedules. For full effectiveness, these (or any other cleaning programme) should be rigorously enforced by senior management in all processing establishments. Weekly cleaning should make a point of including less accessible areas, possibly overlooked during daily clean-ups.

General note
An effective detergent or detergent/disinfectant must be quickly and completely soluble in water. It must have the ability to soften water and have a good wetting or penetrating action on soiled surfaces.

An emulsifying effect on fat and dissolving action on meat particles is also required, together with a subsequent suspending action. Good rinsing properties are necessary to ensure there are no detergent residues.

NOTIFIABLE DISEASES

Any notifiable disease must be immediately reported to the Police, the Ministry of Agriculture, Fisheries & Food (in Scotland the Scottish Office Agriculture, Environment and Fisheries Department), the Divisional Veterinary Officer, the Animal Health Inspector and, in the case of Anthrax, the Consultant in Communicable Disease Control (formerly the Medical Officer for Environmental Health).

The following diseases of deer are notifiable:

Bovine tuberculosis
Foot and mouth disease
Anthrax

The following diseases of wild boar are notifiable:

Foot and mouth disease
Classical swine fever
African swine fever
Swine vesicular disease
Anthrax

DISPOSAL OF GRALLOCH AND ANIMAL BY-PRODUCTS

The Animal By-Products Order 1999 requires animal by-products (as defined in article 3) to be disposed of by one of the following methods:

1. rendering in approved premises,
2. incineration,
3. burial.

The previous Order in 1992 raised concerns that the gralloch or rabbits shot and left on the land may be classed as animal by-products and would need appropriate disposal.

However Article 3(3c) of the 1999 Order states that it shall not apply to a by-product from a wild mammal or wild bird other than one produced in premises used for processing mammals or birds. In effect this means that the stalker or pest controller is not required to dispose of gralloch, head or legs or rabbit carcases where this takes place in the field. Where carcases are taken to a larder for processing by gralloching, skinning, leg or head removal the by-products must be disposed of under the conditions of the Order. The full Order is available free on the internet via www.hmso.gov.uk and advice should be sought from the local authority which enforces the Order.

LEGISLATION ASSOCIATED WITH VENISON DEALING

Apart from the Acts referred to throughout this chapter, there is a variety of other legislation which affects those who deal in venison. The following table summarises the main provisions.

Legislation	Those affected	Implications/descriptions
Game Act, 1831 Deer Acts	Whole trade	Close seasons. Restrictions on sales.
Animal Health Act, 1981	Whole trade	Any notifiable disease must be reported.
Food Safety Act, 1990	Game/venison dealers, processors and shops	Hygiene requirements for food, including game meat.
Food Premises (Registration) Regulations, 1991	Game processors and game larder operators where the premises are not approved under the Wild Game Meat (Hygiene and Inspection) Regulations, 1995	Premises used for a food business on five or more days in any five consecutive weeks should be registered with the local authority at least twenty-eight days beforehand.
Fresh Meat (Hygiene and Inspection) Regulations, 1995	Deer farms (not park deer)	Hygiene regulations similar to those for red meat industry. Costs of upgrading and of veterinary inspection borne by the dealers.

Legislation	Those affected	Implications/descriptions
Wild Game Meat (Hygiene and Inspection) Regulations,1995 implementing, in part, the E.C. Wild Game Directive in the U.K.	All Game/venison dealers and processors handling product destined for export to other member states or to be E.C. health marked for commercial reasons (e.g. supply to major U.K. retailers)	Requirements specific to the game industry. Premises, personal hygiene, meat handling and storage all specified in detail. Regular veterinary inspection. Costs of upgrading and inspection to be borne by dealers.
	Stalker	Deer offal to be kept with carcase.
	Exporters	Provisions for large game to be exported in skin (also in chilled, not frozen form).
Animal By-Products (Identification) Regulations, 1995 and associated Order	Game processors	Imposes a requirement to sterilise or stain certain unfit by-products of processing
Products of Animal Origin (Import and Export) Regulations, 1996	Exporters	Make it an offence to export game to other member states except in accordance with Fresh Meat or Wild Game Meat requirements. Game must be accompanied by documentation required by the regulation or by the member state of destination
Deer Act, 1991 Deer (Scotland) act, 1996 Game Act, 1831/1832 Game Licenses Act, 1860		Licenses to kill/deal in game and deer issued by post offices and local authorities.

CHAPTER 6

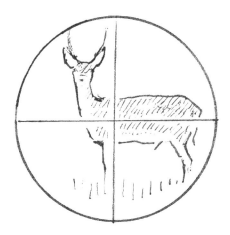

The Use of Firearms for Deer

Deer have no natural predators in this country and therefore their numbers must be regulated and kept in balance with the environment. The most effective and humane way for this to be done is by the proper and careful use of firearms. Whether it is done by the professional or recreational stalker matters not: one standard of proficiency applies. The safety of the public, domestic animals and the humane killing of deer are the main considerations of deer management involving the use of firearms.

Historically, deer have been shot with all types of weapons. Many of these have been unsuitable and much unnecessary suffering has been caused. Many deer, particularly roe, were shot with shotguns during what were known as 'deer drives'. Through education and best practice, this has now ceased and the use of shotguns or other unsuitable weapons would now be illegal in these circumstances.[59]

The high-velocity rifle has emerged over the years as the most effective firearm for use against deer. When used with a telescopic sight, calibrated to the point of aim (zeroed), it can be devastatingly

---

59. See chapters 2 and 3 for the circumstances in which shotguns can be used.

accurate over a considerable distance. Provided the bullet is correctly placed, deer can be shot humanely with little damage to the venison.

LEGISLATION

The legislation governing firearms and their use has to strike a balance of protecting the public against their misuse on the one hand, and allowing legitimate users to own and have easy access to rifles on the other. Ignorance and misunderstanding abound on the subject of the ownership and use of firearms. The two terrible but isolated tragedies arising from their misuse in recent years have highlighted the problems of achieving the right balance between restriction and access for legitimate use.

There has been a raft of gun control laws from 1509 onwards, but the first modern Firearms Act was introduced in 1920, prior to which there was little effective control on their possession. Subsequent legislation has introduced provisions to control the use of certain firearms in the interest of public safety. This is reflected in the control of the more powerful weapons, the restrictions on young persons, and the provisions against the use of firearms in the commission of crime. In recent years the number of certificate holders has virtually halved from 256,000 in 1968 to 133,000 in 1997. Despite the tight controls, which often penalise the legitimate stalker, the criminal use of un-licensed firearms continues. Rifles, apart from those chambered for low-powered .22 inch rimfire ammunition feature very little in criminal offences.[60]

Current legislation is complex, with a number of Acts that generate new provisions and amendments to the original Act. The danger here is that those who manage deer, either professionally or as a sport, are likely to fall foul of the law due to the confusion created by its complexity. Nevertheless, of course, ignorance of the law is no excuse.

The Firearms Act, 1968 (which applies to England, Wales and Scotland) is the main statute governing the possession, control and use of firearms. The Firearms Rules, 1989, prescribed the form of firearm and shotgun certificates and detailed the conditions under which firearm certificates are held. These rules were replaced by the Firearms Rules, 1998.

The Firearms (Amendment) Act, 1988, substantially amended the main statute, bringing stricter controls particularly in relation to

---

60. T. A. Warlow, *Science and Justice* 1996 36(1) 55–58.

the ownership of shotguns, which were redefined by the Act. The provisions of the European Weapons Directive were absorbed into U.K. legislation in 1992. The main changes were additions to the list of prohibited weapons, restrictions on use by people under 18 years, controls on sale and purchase in countries within the European Union and the introduction of the European Firearms Pass (E.F.P.).

The Firearms (Amendment) Act, 1997, was speedily introduced following an urgent review of firearm controls in which the Government took cognisance of Lord Cullen's Report of the Public Inquiry into the Shootings at Dunblane Primary School. The Act introduced tighter controls, which included a general prohibition on handguns. In addition, deer stalkers were affected by the prohibition of expanding ammunition.

Northern Ireland has its own separate legislation and the main provisions affecting stalkers are contained within the Firearms (Northern Ireland) Order, 1981. This legislation is similar in parts to that contained within the Firearms Act, 1968. Where there are differences which may affect the stalker these are elaborated upon within the text.

The Firearms Consultative Committee (F.C.C.)

The Firearms (Amendment) Act, 1988, section 22(1), provided for the establishment of this independent body to keep under review the working of the Firearms Acts. The Committee, consisting of a chairman and not less than twelve other members, is appointed by the Secretary of State. The members selected must have knowledge and experience of firearms, weapon technology or the administration or enforcement of firearm legislation.

The continued existence, make-up and future role of this important body is uncertain. Of particular note to deer stalkers are the supportive views of the F.C.C., which have been expressed to the government in respect of expanding ammunition and the use of pistols for the humane dispatch of animals. In its ninth report for example, it recommended:

> In the light of the general ban on handguns, the Government should consider whether the ban on expanding ammunition serves any useful purpose and, if not, its repeal.

The subject of the use of both expanding ammunition and handguns by those involved with the management of deer is dealt with in detail later.

The requirement for a firearm certificate

The legislation creates different controls and licensing requirements for certain types of firearm and ammunition defined by the Firearms Acts, 1968 to 1997. Three main classes of firearm exist:

- firearms (section 1)
- shotguns (section 2)
- prohibited weapons (section 5)

Some weapons are defined as 'firearms' but may not need to be licensed – e.g. air weapons that are not declared specially dangerous, or firearms regarded as antiques. But all firearms that can be legally used for deer require a valid firearm certificate. Shotguns can be used in specified circumstances, and a valid shotgun certificate is required. Firearm certificate applications and the exemptions that apply are detailed later in the chapter.

What is a firearm?

The use of firearms against deer is strictly regulated by deer legislation, which lays down both permitted and prohibited weapons and ammunition, and these are elaborated upon later. For the purposes of firearm legislation, a 'firearm' is defined as follows (section 57(1) Firearms Act, 1968, and Article 2(2) Firearms (Northern Ireland) Order, 1981):

> A lethal-barrelled weapon of any description from which any shot, bullet or other missile can be discharged and includes:

(a) any prohibited weapon (whether lethal or not); and
(b) any component part of such a lethal or prohibited weapon; and
(c) any accessory to any such weapons designed or adapted to diminish the noise or flash caused by firing the weapon.

In addition to this definition case law provides further guidance in cases which have been disputed.

A **'lethal-barrelled'** weapon is one capable of causing injury from which death may result. It follows that the majority of weapons are going to fall into this class, including air weapons. A signal pistol has been held to be a firearm although it was never designed to injure or kill.[61] The description 'barrelled' requires the weapon to have some

61. Read v. Donovan (1947) KB826.

form of cylinder or tube from which a projectile can be discharged. Hence a crossbow is not classed as a firearm.[62]

A firearm can be **'discharged'** by any means, including gunpowder, gas, spring and air pressure. It is not essential that the weapon is capable of firing ammunition. If it can be quickly and readily converted to enable firing then it may be classed as a 'firearm' for the purposes of the Acts.[63] See also section 1(1)(b) Firearms Act, 1982; the test is that no special skill is required on the part of the person doing the conversion, and that ordinary tools for home D.I.Y. work can be used.

The term **'prohibited weapon'** is defined under section 5(1), Firearms Act, 1968, as amended[64] as:

(1)   Any firearm so designed or adapted that two or more missiles can be successfully discharged without repeated pressure on the trigger.

(2)   Any self-loading or pump-action rifled gun other than .22 rim-fire.

(3)   Any firearm which either has a barrel less than 30cm or is less than 60cm overall, other than an air weapon, a muzzle-loading gun or a firearm designed as signalling apparatus.

(4)   Any self-loading or pump-action smooth-bore gun (not an air weapon or .22 rim-fire) with either barrel less than 24 inches or overall length less than 40 inches.

(5)   Any smooth-bore revolver gun (not 9mm rim-fire or a muzzle-loading gun).

(6)   Any rocket launcher or mortar.

(7)   Any firearm which is disguised as another object e.g. walking stick (unless regarded as an antique).

The term **'component part'** relates only to the parts of a firearm that are pressure bearing from the force of the explosion like the barrel, bolt or action. Items such as telescopic sights, which are normally regarded as accessories, may be referred to as component parts but because they are not essential to the firing of the weapon their possession, purchase or sale are not restricted and do not require to be entered on a firearm certificate.[65] However, any device

---

62. Restrictions on sale and use of crossbows by juveniles are set out in the Crossbows Act, 1987. See chapter 9 for a discussion of their use in poaching.
63. Cafferata v. Wilson (1936) All E.R. 149.
64. Firearms Act, 1988, Amendment Regulations, 1992, and Firearm (Amendment) Act, 1997
65. Watson v. Herman (1952) 2 All E.R. 70.

designed to diminish the noise or flash of a weapon, such as a sound moderator (silencer), is required to be included on a firearm certificate whether it is fitted to a weapon or held separately. Certificates are not required for sound moderators for shotguns or air weapons.

'**Ammunition**' includes ammunition for any firearm as well as grenades, bombs etc., whether capable of use with a firearm or not. It is generally accepted to include four components; projectile, charge, primer and case.

The definition of '**prohibited ammunition**' will be of interest to stalkers as, following the introduction of the Firearms (Amendment) Act, 1997, this now includes a general prohibition on expanding ammunition and missiles. However, its use against deer is obligatory, and it is catered for within the exemptions as elaborated upon later.

Under section 5(1) as amended, prohibited ammunition is defined as:

- any cartridge or bullet designed to explode[66] on or immediately before impact
- any ammunition containing any noxious liquid, gas or other thing
- if capable of use with a firearm any grenade, bomb, rocket or shell designed to explode
- any ammunition which incorporates a missile designed or adapted to expand on impact (expanding ammunition)

66. This refers to a form of explosive charge within the projectile as opposed to expanding-type bullets.

PERMITTED FIREARMS AND AMMUNITION FOR DEER

It is essential for those who shoot deer to be familiar with the Deer Acts applicable to the countries in which they intend to shoot. The Acts stipulate not only the firearms and ammunition that are permitted for use against deer, but also those that are prohibited.

Some fundamental differences exist between the Acts in the specification of rifles and ammunition. In England and Wales it will be noted that it is the *calibre* of the weapon and its *muzzle energy* that are the main criteria for lawful use. In Scotland the criteria relate to the *ammunition, muzzle energy* and *velocity*. It would therefore be legal to use any rifle capable of firing that ammunition with the required power. In Northern Ireland it is a combination of both rifle calibre, ammunition and muzzle energy. The result is that certain weapons may be legal on one side of the border but not the other, which is by no means ideal for the stalker who shoots in both England and Scotland; for example .22 centre-fire cartridges (minimum .222 Remington but not the Hornet) can only be used in Scotland, and then only for roe.

The following chart, which consolidates the provisions, is provided for ease of reference. The circumstances in which shotguns may be used are shown and these should be read in conjunction with chapter 4 on crop damage.

Firearms permitted for killing deer in England, Wales, Northern Ireland and Scotland

ENGLAND AND WALES	
Rifles:	Calibre of not less than .240 in or muzzle energy of not less than 1700 ft/lb
Rifle ammunition:	Bullet must be soft-nosed or hollow-nosed
Shotgun:	Not less than 12-bore. A shotgun may be used only by the occupier and certain others, who must be able to prove serious damage (see Deer Act, 1991, section 7)
Shotgun ammunition:	Rifled slug of not less than 22.68 g (350 grains) or AAA shot
Prohibitions:	Any air gun, air rifle or air pistol

NORTHERN IRELAND

Rifles:	Calibre of not less than .236 in (6 mm)
Rifle ammunition:	Muzzle energy of not less than 1700 ft/lb (2305 joules)
	Bullet of not less than 6.48 g (100 grains)
	Expanding bullets designed to deform in predictable manner
Shotguns:	Not less than 12-bore. A shotgun may be used only by the occupier and certain others, who must be able to prove serious damage (see Wildlife (Northern Ireland) Order, 1985, section 20)
Shotgun ammunition:	Rifled slug of not less than 22.68 g (350 grains) or AAA shot
Prohibitions:	Any air gun, air rifle, air pistol or gas-propelled weapon; any pistol, revolver or handgun other than slaughtering instrument

SCOTLAND

Rifle ammunition:	**Roe deer:**	Bullets of not less than 50 grains AND Muzzle velocity of not less than 2450 ft per sec. AND Muzzle energy of not less than 1000 ft/lb
	All deer:	Bullets of not less than 100 grains AND Muzzle velocity of not less than 2450 ft per sec. AND Muzzle energy of not less than 1750 ft/lb
	Expanding bullets designed to deform in predictable manner	
Shotguns:	Not less than 12-bore. A shotgun may be used only by the occupier and certain others, who must be able to prove serious damage (see Deer (Firearms etc.) (Scotland) Order, 1985, No. 1168)	
Shotgun ammunition:	**All deer:**	Rifled slug of not less than 380 grains or shot not smaller than SSG
	Roe deer:	Shot not smaller than AAA
Prohibitions:	Any sight specially designed for night shooting	

101

Calibre

As the development of firearms evolved, a classification was introduced according to the size of the bore of the gun barrel – the nominal
diameter of the bore measured across the lands, expressed in decimal
points of an inch for British and American guns, and millimetres for
Continental guns. The measurement became known as the *calibre* of
the weapon.

Muzzle energy

Muzzle energy is calculated from the formula:

$$\frac{\text{bullet weight} \times (\text{muzzle velocity})^2}{\text{acceleration of gravity } (450,400)}$$

For example a 150-grain bullet with a muzzle velocity of 2800 ft per
sec. (.270 Winchester) would have a calculated muzzle energy of:

$$\frac{150 \times 2800 \times 2800}{450,400} = 2611 \text{ ft lb}$$

If there is any doubt as to whether a particular combination of rifle
and bullet meets the required ballistic performance as given above,
then advice should be sought from a reputable firearms dealer or the
manufacturer. Alternatively the Deer Commission for Scotland and
the B.A.S.C. Deer Officer can be consulted.[67]

Expanding ammunition

Section 10 of the Firearms (Amendment) Act, 1997, creates a
number of exemptions in respect of the use of expanding ammunition. Its possession, purchase or acquisition must be authorised by
a firearm certificate or visitor's firearm permit, which should contain
a condition restricting the expanding ammunition to use in connection with any one or more of the following activities:

- the lawful shooting of deer
- the shooting of vermin or, in the course of carrying on activities in
  connection with the management of any estate, other wildlife
- the humane killing of animals

67. See page 203 for contact details.

- the shooting of animals for the protection of other animals or humans

We must stress that this exemption applies only to the requirement of authority under section 5, and that a firearm certificate under section 1 is still required and must contain the condition referred to above. The exemption not only caters for the ammunition's use in deer shooting but also for its use in activities *connected with* deer shooting. Without strict legal guidance or a court ruling, the words 'in connection with' are open to different interpretations by different licensing authorities. It is clear from the debate that took place during the preparation of the legislation that it was the government's intention to ensure that the use of expanding ammunition catered for the preparatory stages that may have to be followed to ensure that deer are shot humanely. As Baroness Blatch stated, 'That includes allowing the certificate holder to zero or adjust the gun sights as well as general testing and practice.'

It is our opinion that any action that is directly related to these activities falls within the exemption, including practising with expanding ammunition at inanimate objects. It should be appreciated that for deer to be shot humanely, accuracy and knowledge of the vital killing areas are essential. This is only possible by ensuring not only that the user is proficient but also that the equipment and ammunition are capable of producing the required ballistic performance. It follows therefore that both practice and the testing of both equipment and ammunition, of the exact type to be used on live deer, is essential.

Stalkers should not be restricted as to how often they practise or what quantities of ammunition they use to achieve accuracy. It should also be appreciated that some individuals will require more practice than others. A check of accuracy may be necessary on a regular basis or as a result of a miss or knock to the sights.

Training and education in stalking competence, which requires the participant to use a rifle and expanding ammunition, should also be seen as preparatory to the humane shooting of deer. However it is not a prerequisite for the grant of a firearm certificate.

Difficulties arise in the interpretation of the exemption when considering whether any type of rifle competition shooting could be classed as being 'in connection with' the lawful shooting of deer. Regional branches of the British Deer Society regularly hold such competitions, and B.A.S.C. considers that they are run in connection with the lawful shooting of deer as they are designed to enhance marksmanship and thus encourage humane shooting.

Generally, competition shooting *per se* would not fall within the criteria. However, there may be situations where the winning of a competition may be shown as ancillary to the test of stalking marks-manship and therefore one may argue this could then be seen as being in connection with the lawful shooting of deer. If it were put to the test, a court would have to decide on the basis of the merits of the individual case, using the natural sense and common use of the words.

The exemption also provides that expanding ammunition may be used for 'the shooting of vermin or, in the course of carrying on activities in connection with the management of any estate, other wildlife'. If you intend to use your rifle in these circumstances your certificate must include this condition, otherwise such use will be unlawful. The shooting of non-target species and wild boar are elaborated upon in chapter 7.

If you are in any doubt as to whether or not your use of expanding ammunition falls within the legal exemption, remember that it is your responsibility to ensure that you comply with the conditions of your certificate; we would therefore advise you to consult the firearms licensing department responsible for issuing your certificate. Alternatively you may contact the Firearms Department at the B.A.S.C. for advice.[68]

Exemptions to prevent suffering

Each of the Acts relating to deer make exceptions for dealing with injured or diseased deer in circumstances where the use of firearms would otherwise be illegal. In Scotland this is extended to cover the prevention of suffering of dependent offspring.

England and Wales (The Deer Act, 1991, section 6(4))
A person will not be guilty of an offence under section 4(2)(a) (the use of prohibited firearms and ammunition) by reason of the use of any smooth-bore gun for the purpose of killing any deer if he shows that the deer had been so seriously injured otherwise than by his unlawful act, or was in such a condition, that to kill it was an act of mercy.

Consequently any shotgun can be used in these circumstances. The exemption refers to section 4(2)(a), which includes shotgun ammunition, and it is our view that the intention here is to allow the use of any appropriate shotgun ammunition. It is stressed that no other prohibited weapons are included in this exemption, so any other firearm and ammunition used in these circumstances must be of a type permitted by the legislation as outlined in the chart on pages

68. See page 203 for contact details.

SWAN HILL PRESS
101 LONGDEN ROAD
SHREWSBURY
SHROPSHIRE SY3 9BR

SWAN·HILL
PRESS

Thank you for buying this Swan Hill Press book. If you would like to be kept informed about our forthcoming publications, please fill in this card.

Name: ....

Address: ....

....

....

1) In order to assist our editors in determining the type of books our readers require could you please tick your areas of interest in the spaces below.

| Fishing ☐ | Field Sports ☐ | Natural History ☐ | Diving ☐ |
| Wildlife Art ☐ | Equestrian ☐ | Decorative Arts ☐ | Climbing ☐ |

2) How did this book come to your notice?
☐ Magazine Advertisement. Which magazine? _____
☐ Book Review. Which publication? _____
☐ In a bookshop. Which bookshop? _____

3) In which Swan Hill Press book did you find this card? _____
(Please specify title)

100 to 101. Confusion has arisen over whether the .22 rim-fire rifle can be used, but this weapon is not exempt, so despite its effectiveness in this situation its use is illegal.

Handguns are not included as prohibited weapons and, provided the appropriate firearm certificate is held, could legitimately be used in these circumstances.[69]

Northern Ireland (The Wildlife (Northern Ireland) Order, 1985)
A person shall not be guilty of an offence under article 19(3)(a) (prohibited firearms and ammunition) by reason of the killing of any deer by using any smooth-bore gun, if he shows that the deer had been so seriously injured, otherwise than by his unlawful act, or was in such a condition, that to kill it was an act of mercy.

This exemption would appear to be identical to that applying in England and Wales outlined above with the exception of the use of handguns, which Schedule 11 of the Act specifically prohibits.

Scotland (The Deer (Firearms etc.) (Scotland) Order, 1985)
A person shall not be guilty of an offence against this Act or any order made under it in respect of any act done for the purpose of preventing suffering by an injured or diseased deer; or a deer calf, fawn or kid deprived, or about to be deprived, of its mother.

The effect of this exemption in relation to the use of firearms, is that any firearm of any description can be used in the circumstances of a mercy killing without contravening the law relating to deer.

The use of handguns for dispatching wounded deer

It will be noted that the use of handguns for the mercy killing of deer is not prohibited by the Deer Acts in England and Wales or Scotland. In addition, an exemption exists under section 3 of the Firearms (Amendment) Act, 1997, in circumstances where an appropriate firearm certificate is held and it is subject to a condition that it is only for use in connection with the humane killing of animals. This has been held to include the humane dispatch of wounded or injured deer.[70] In applying for such a certificate you are required to demonstrate that you have a good reason for possessing a handgun for this purpose and chief constables must consider cases on their individual merits. In the case of Hughes v. The Chief Constable of South Wales, 1998, the appeal was dismissed on the basis that the court was not satisfied that the appellant's reason for retention of a .38 Smith &

69. The licensing and use of handguns is discussed on page 106.
70. Goodman & Newton v. The Chief Constable of Derbyshire 1998.

Wesson six-shot revolver was for the humane destruction of animals. Association of Chief Police Officer guidance is that the preferred option is a .32 single-shot pistol.

Carrying a handgun in addition to a rifle, for the sole purpose of dispatching a wounded beast, is frowned upon by many experienced stalkers. The late John Hodgkiss, with whom we regularly exchanged legal views, summed up our thoughts in a letter on the subject:

> The question of applications for firearm certificates for pistols for destroying deer which have been wounded during the course of stalking continues to arise. Allow me, please, to be categoric about this. Whilst even the most experienced and conscientious stalker will, alas, sooner or later fail to kill a deer outright, such a situation should occur only as an extreme exception. Even then, with proper fieldcraft – and, ideally, the use of a trained dog – the animal will always be tracked down and dispatched (with rifle or, if needs be, the customary *coup de grace*). There is NO case for the use of handguns (of any calibre).
>
> In this country deer are big game and should be regarded as such, and frankly, any person who cannot attain the standards implied in the previous paragraph should not go out after deer. Any applicant must make sure as humanly as possible that he kills cleanly with the first shot or only stalks in the company of a competent stalker or ceases to stalk until he is able to do so on his own, proficiently, responsibly and safely. In any case, handguns of all types are far from easy to handle accurately and reliably even after considerable practice, and their use would be even more precarious in the case of a wounded deer which may be struggling or in an awkward position.[71]

Whilst many people view the handgun as being an unnecessary appendage when stalking there are situations where its use is appropriate and 'good reason' should not be difficult to establish. Many deer managers and rangers are regularly called out, often by the police, to deal with casualties. In this situation, where the beast is under some control, the use of a handgun is justified. The issue of a certificate for such use should additionally cater for the dispatching of wounded deer trapped in fences or disabled by farm machinery etc.[72]

71. Letter to the authors, dated 20 September 1990, from the late John Hodgkiss, past Vice-president of the British Deer Society and the Chairman of the Federation of Deer Management Societies.
72. Liabilities in respect of the humane dispatch of deer are covered in chapter 7.

There are situations where the use of handguns is appropriate.

FIREARM CERTIFICATES

All firearms that are permitted for use against deer fall within the scope of section 1 of the Firearms Act, 1968, and if you wish to acquire, possess or use such weapons a firearm certificate is required. The exception is the conditional use of shotguns, for which a shotgun certificate is required.[73]

The term 'possession' should be viewed in its widest possible sense. It includes not only physical possession but also 'constructive' possession – e.g. where the firearm is in a house or vehicle under the control of a person who is aware of its presence.[74] One aspect of possession was considered in Hall v. Cotton and Treadwell (1986).[75] Here the learned judge said:

> Cases of momentary delivery of a shotgun to another person in for example, a temporary emergency, or for the purpose of inspection, could hardly be said to have involved either a transfer by the deliveror or the taking of possession by the deliveree; equally, a spouse or servant temporarily entrusted with the custody of a shotgun by its owner would in normal circumstances be regarded as the owner's agent; there would thus be no transfer by the latter, nor acceptance of any more than the barest custody by the former . . .'

73. See the chart on pages 100–101 and chapter 4 on crop damage.
74. Sullivan v. Earl of Caithness (1976) 1 All E.R.
75. 83 Cr. App. R 257.

This tends to mitigate against the excesses of a strict interpretation of 'possession'.

Exemptions

There are numerous exemptions to the requirement for firearm certificates both in terms of types of weapons and circumstances of use. The following have been selected as being of relevance to stalkers and deer managers.

The 'estate rifle'

The Firearms (Amendment) Act, 1988, made provision for the use of what is commonly and erroneously referred to as the 'estate rifle'. Section 16 states that a rifle may be borrowed, by a person aged 17 or over, from the occupier of private premies (which includes land) and used on those premises in the presence of the occupier or his employee providing the latter holds the appropriate firearm certificate, but the rifle and ammunition can only be used in accordance with the conditions of that certificate. Ammunition may also be purchased or acquired under this exemption. In practice, this is normally acquired direct from the owner of the rifle, and in these circumstances the transaction would not need to be entered on the certificate. Any remaining surplus ammunition should remain with the certificate holder. It must be stressed that where a rifle is used in the presence of the employee, the employee himself must possess a certificate covering his use of it.

The term 'occupier' is not defined in this context by the Act, and in the absence of a legal ruling, it is open to interpretation. Occupation of land must be broad in nature and enforceable through the courts, it is generally accepted that it would include a person who holds the sporting rights to deer.

This exemption is of particular benefit to visitors from abroad or those who wish to stalk occasionally without the need or expense of purchasing a rifle and obtaining a certificate.

Carrying a firearm for the certificate holder

A person may carry, but not use, a firearm or ammunition belonging to another person without the need for a firearm certificate, provided it is for the certificate holder's use and under his instruction and for a sporting purpose only.[76] This is normally interpreted as applying to gun bearers, loaders etc.

Crown servants

Crown servants are allowed to possess, purchase or acquire firearms and ammunition in connection with their business or occupation. As Crown servants, the Forestry Commission rangers who use firearms in their work are covered by the Crown exemption. However, any personal firearms that they may hold must be covered by a firearm certificate.

Shotguns

A shotgun certificate is not required where a person borrows a shotgun from the occupier of private premises, provided it is used on those premises and in his presence.

Restrictions on young persons

Children under fourteen cannot possess section 1 firearms or ammunition. It is an offence to make a gift of or lend a firearm to a child, or to part with possession to a child unless he is carrying it for, and under the instruction of, the owner who is the holder of an appropriate certificate and using it for sporting purposes.

Young people between the ages of fourteen and seventeen are not permitted to purchase or hire any firearms or ammunition. However provided they hold a valid firearm certificate they may possess and use section 1 firearms and ammunition in accordance with the terms of the certificate. They can only acquire such weapons by gift or loan where both parties possess firearm certificates authorising the transaction.

76. Shooting rats is not a sporting purpose – Morton v. Chaney (1960) 3 All E.R. 632.

Different regulations apply in Northern Ireland. The Firearms (Northern Ireland) Order, 1981, article 26, states:

(1)   Except as provided by paragraphs (3) and (4) anyone under 18 years of age who purchases, acquires or has in their possession a firearm or ammunition, shall be guilty of an offence.

(2)   A person who sells or transfers a firearm or ammunition to any person prohibited by this article from possessing such firearm or ammunition, shall be guilty of an offence.

(3)   It is *not* an offence for any person to have in their possession a firearm or ammunition if –

   (a)   they show that under the Order they are entitled to possess without holding a firearm certificate
   (b)   they show that they are entitled to possess by virtue of article 15 (they possess firearm or shotgun certificates granted in Great Britain).

(4)   It is *not* an offence for a person age 16 years or above to –
   (a)   have a firearm or ammunition for sporting purposes where he is in the company and under supervision of another person not under 18 years of age, who holds a firearm certificate for the firearm and ammunition; or
   (b)   purchase, acquire or possess a shotgun, or any other firearm not exceeding .22 calibre, and ammunition therefore for the purpose of destroying or controlling animals and birds on either agricultural land occupied by him or on which he works and also resides.

Application for the grant of a certificate

If you wish to acquire, possess or use any firearm or ammunition to which section 1 of the Act applies, unless one of the exemptions applies you must first obtain a firearm certificate from the chief officer of police for the area in which you reside. A certificate will be granted if the chief officer is satisfied that the applicant has good reason for requiring the weapon and that there is no danger to public safety or the peace. Discretion to grant or refuse an application rests with that chief officer, in whom is vested the responsibility to ensure that a certificate is not granted to a person of intemperate habits or unsound mind, or who for any reason is unfitted to be entrusted with a firearm.

There is a right of appeal to the Crown or Sheriff Court against a refusal to grant or renew a certificate and or the revocation of a certificate.[77] If you are dissatisfied with the decision we recommend that you seek early advice from a solicitor well versed in such matters. Alternatively if you are a member of the B.A.S.C. you should contact their Firearms Department. Notice of appeals must be made within twenty-one days of receipt of the chief officer's notice of decision, unless leave has been sought to appeal out of time.

Certificates are issued in the form of a folding booklet and specify either the number of firearms possessed or the number which may be acquired, or both. There is no limit on the number of firearms that can be held but a good reason must be demonstrated in respect of each weapon. It is usual for deer stalkers to possess more than one calibre of weapon and good reason can be made out on the basis of the species of deer to be shot or the nature of the stalking terrain. For example a smaller calibre may be requested for roe, and the stutzen-type rifle for woodland. Stated on the certificate will be the amount of ammunition which may be possessed at any one time and the amount which may be purchased. Subsequent purchases of firearms or ammunition over the initial number authorised must only take place following a variation of the certificate.

Conditions

The Firearms Rules, 1998, impose the following statutory conditions on certificate holders:

- The holder must, on receipt of the certificate, sign it in ink
- Firearms and ammunition must be kept in a secure place
- Any theft, loss, destruction or deactivation of a firearm must be reported to the police
- Any change of permanent address must be notified to the police

Additional conditions may be imposed by the chief officer at his discretion. These may relate to where the firearms are to be kept, or restrict where and under what circumstances they may be used. The chief officer may at any time vary such conditions and can require the production of the certificate within twenty-one days for this purpose. A certificate may be revoked if it is not produced, and there is no appeal in these circumstances.

---

77. There is no right of appeal against a chief officer's decision not to vary the conditions – R. v. Cambridge Court, Ex Parte Buckland (1968).

Completion of the form

Application forms (form 101) are obtainable from police stations. The same form is used for the grant, renewal and variation of a certificate. Once issued the certificate will last for a period of five years; prior to expiry it will be necessary to apply for renewal. The form makes provision for you to request a shotgun certificate to run coterminously with the firearm certificate. The shotgun certificate will expire on the same day as the firearm certificate. If both applications are dealt with at the same time the fee payable for the grant or renewal of the shotgun certificate will normally be less.

The form is generally self-explanatory and is split into sections, A–F, to cater for varying applications. Explanatory notes are included on the reverse side of the form and cover most of the common queries raised. If difficulty is experienced in completion of any part of the form we recommend that you contact your local licensing department or firearms licensing officer. If you are a B.A.S.C. member you can also contact the B.A.S.C. Firearms Department.

Previous convictions
You are required in law to reveal whether or not you have been convicted of any offence. You are not entitled to withhold such information, which includes motoring offences and convictions outside Great Britain. Convictions that are classed as 'spent' under the Rehabilitation of Offenders Act, 1974, are also required to be declared. Both a conditional discharge and an absolute discharge, but not a caution, count as convictions for this purpose. (On renewal or variation, details need only be given of convictions since the existing certificate was issued.)

Choice of weapon
Where a firearm is to be purchased or acquired it is not necessary for the make and identification number of the weapon to be stated on the form, as this is unlikely to be known at the time of application. Such details would be required to be endorsed on the certificate by the seller or giver, who will first check that the certificate authorises you to possess that type of weapon. It is not unusual for stalkers to be uncertain when choosing a calibre. There is considerable choice and much debate on the virtues of the calibres permitted for use against deer. If you are unsure and wish to press ahead with your application your licensing department may accept an application requesting authorisation to possess a rifle between certain calibres – e.g. .243–.308 – rather than restricting your choice. However you should clarify this at the time as not all licensing departments permit

this, some require you state a specific calibre. Such details would subsequently be entered on the certificate at the time of purchase or acquisition (table 1 on the back of the certificate).

Ammunition
The amount of ammunition you ask to purchase and possess needs to be appropriate to your intended use of the weapon. Applications are judged on an individual basis and chief officers are asked to be flexible and pay due regard to the needs of the applicant.

You should ensure that you have catered for the amount you may need to use on zeroing and practice, particularly if a new firearm or telescopic sight has been purchased. By comparison the amount used on actually shooting deer is usually quite small. The quantity you request to possess at any one time should be considerably greater than the amount to be purchased, in order to allow for an operating surplus.

If you load your own ammunition you will need to take account of the quantities you may wish to load at any one time. You will also need to include a separate quantity for expanding bullets (or missiles) which are now classed as ammunition in their own right and count towards the allocation on the certificate. The application form requests the inclusion of expanding ammunition and expanding missiles. Some licensing departments have recognised the distinction between expanding bullets/missiles and loaded cartridges and have set two levels of authority on certificates where requested. It is usually more economical to purchase expanding bullets in large quantities which are often packaged in minimum lots of 100. It should be appreciated therefore that the quantity of loaded cartridges by comparison will be much lower.

The Control of Explosives Regulations, 1991 (C.O.E.R.) provide exemptions for private use of up to 5 kg of smokeless powder (U.N. 0160 & 0161) used for the reloading of rifle ammunition. The storage of over 5 kg of these smokeless powders require licensing with the local authority under the Explosives Act, 1875. The acquisition of primers is subject to an exemption order, but they are included in the total amount of explosive allowed to be kept without licence (the explosive content of a typical cartridge primer is approximately .8 grain).

C.O.E.R. permits the keeping of small-arms ammunition/primers (cartridges made-up in assembled form) of up to 15 kg. This allows for all normal quantities of cartridges required by stalkers to be stored. In calculating the amount of ammunition you may keep, it is the net weight of powder and primer components that is used rather than the total weight of the cartridges.

The amount of non-expanding bullets/missiles you may keep is not restricted and these items do not require to be shown on your firearm application form.

Reason for requiring the firearm and place of intended use
In stating the reason for the use of a firearm stalkers should give careful consideration to both the species to be shot and the place they wish to stalk. The terms 'deer stalking', 'the lawful shooting of deer' and 'deer control' or 'culling' all adequately describe the intended purpose, provided they take account of the Deer Acts with regard to permitted firearms and ammunition. No further description of the intended use should normally be necessary. However there are weapons for which you may need to be specific in stating your intended quarry – e.g. .22 centre-fire for roe deer in Scotland. You should remember to state that you will require to zero the rifle in addition to the sporting purpose stated.

If you wish to take the opportunity to shoot species other than deer, such as wild goats or foxes, you should enter these on the form, otherwise you will not be authorised for such use of the weapon. The situation with feral wild boar is dealt with in chapter 7.

The majority of certificates for stalking rifles will have territorial restrictions, particularly for a first-time applicant who may find a condition restricting him to one approved area. Generally, whilst the certificate will detail the place of use requested on the initial application, it should provide for the holder to shoot elsewhere on condition that permission with that class of firearm has been given by the person who owns the shooting rights or from whom they may be leased or otherwise obtained. The effect of this condition quite rightly puts the

responsibility on the *user* of the firearm to make his own judgement on where it is safe to shoot deer at a particular place. In the right circumstances even a garden may be safe and in the wrong circumstances the open hill may be equally unsafe. It should be stressed that if a firearm is used recklessly or without due regard to suitable back-stops then nowhere in the country is safe.

In providing details of the place you intend to use the weapon, or have been invited to shoot, you should bear in mind that this will be verified independently by the police, who may also examine the land. Police contact with the landowner, agent or host may come as a surprise if you have not informed them in advance that there may be an approach. This can be embarrassing and may jeopardise your future stalking opportunities. It is also an offence to knowingly or recklessly make a false statement for the grant, renewal or variation of a certificate.

Storage of firearm and ammunition

You are required to give the address at which the firearms and ammunition concerned are to be stored and whether they are to be stored in a British standard (B.S.) gun cabinet.

Under the Firearms Rules, 1989, a safe-keeping condition is attached to all firearm and shotgun certificates. This stipulates that when not in use they must at all times be stored securely so as to prevent, so far as is reasonably practicable, access to the firearms or ammunition by unauthorised persons (the condition does not apply to shotgun ammunition other than solid slug).

The Firearms Rules do not prescribe how firearms must be kept securely. The Home Departments' guidance recommends that you store them in a locked gun cabinet or other similarly secure container. In some cases, if you do not have a gun cabinet, it may be acceptable to remove the firing mechanism from the firearm and store it in a secure container. A securely built gun room or cellar with a steel door that locks can be an acceptable form of secure storage. Ideally section 1 ammunition should be stored in a separate secure compartment within a gun cabinet or in its own secure container, such as a safe.

When considering whether your storage arrangements are secure enough, a chief officer must look at the circumstances of each case and at the overall security arrangements of the premises and, if relevant, the vehicle in which they are transported.

If you fit a gun cabinet you should ensure that it is bolted securely to the wall, sufficient to prevent it being prised off with a crow-bar or garden spade. Ideally it should be positioned in your property out of sight of ground-floor windows. It is not compulsory to have a cabinet which meets the British standard. However, advice on specification is published in the Home Departments' *Firearm Security* leaflet which can be obtained from your local licensing department, which will also offer crime-prevention advice if requested.

The police may wish to inspect your security arrangements, and whilst they do not have the power to do so there would appear little point in refusing to co-operate and delaying the processing of your application.

Security and storage in Northern Ireland
Police policy in relation to deer stalking under the Firearms (Northern Ireland) Order, 1981, should be noted. The bolt for a rifle must generally be stored separately from the weapon and, unless you are classed as a professional gamekeeper or stalker, it must be kept at a police station. You must then apply in writing to the Chief Constable if you intend to go stalking, stating dates, times and locations. Areas are then checked for safety and permission granted or refused. In effect this is the authority for the removal of the bolt from police safe-keeping.

There are some estates which have estate rifles and these can be used by anyone who is deemed competent to use them under supervision of estate employees. The competency qualification currently required is the Deer Stalking Certificate.[78]

Referees
You must provide the names and addresses of two people who have agreed to act as referees for your application. If it is a new application then both referees must have known you for at least two years. They must be resident in Great Britain and must not be members of your immediate family. References must be given freely without payment. Applications for variation only do not require referees.

Renewal and variation of certificates

The renewal and variation procedures are similar to that for the grant of a certificate and as with the grant, form 101 must be completed. Prior to renewal it is usual practice for the issuing licensing department to send you a reminder. However, this is not obligatory and it remains your responsibility to ensure that you apply for renewal in good time. It can be expected, in normal circumstances, that on first renewal your territorial condition will be extended to include other land over which you have permission to shoot with that class of

78. See chapter 7, pages 126 and 127.

firearm. The onus is very much on you then to decide whether it is safe to shoot at a particular location.

If you wish to vary your certificate by the addition of other firearms or some other change, then provided this is done at the time of a renewal no fee will apply. A change to the quantities of ammunition attracts no fee at any time. However, when variations to increase the number of firearms held are applied for at times other than renewal, a fee will be charged, unless it is a 'one for one' transaction. Such a change would be free of charge provided both elements of the variation took place at the same time. If there is a significant gap between the removal of one firearm and its replacement by another, the second variation would be subject to the usual fee, as the number of firearms to which the certificate relates would be increased. The removal of a firearm from a certificate does not attract a fee.

SECURITY OF FIREARMS AND AMMUNITION

Do not underestimate your liabilities regarding the security of your firearms, ammunition and equipment, particularly if you are in the process of insuring them against loss. Whilst you may be able to safeguard your interests by insuring against public liability, loss or theft, you cannot insure against the possible revocation of your firearm certificate through a breach of security conditions. There are also, of course, wider implications as the loss of firearms may result in their use by criminals, although the risk is not as great with sporting rifles as it is with handguns or shotguns.

Stalkers need to be security conscious. The safe-keeping condition that appears on firearm certificates gives clear guidance:

> The firearms and ammunition to which this certificate relates must at all times . . . be stored securely so as to prevent, so far as is reasonably practicable, access to the firearms or ammunition by an unauthorised person.

The courts are reluctant to convict defendants who have complied with Home Departments' guidance, and it would also be difficult to justify the revocation of a firearm certificate if the holder was seen to have followed the guidance. Nevertheless, any additional security above this minimum level must be beneficial. And the condition has wide-ranging implications, as stalking often involves being away from home in remote areas, where the normal security arrangements are not available.

It may be useful to consider the security implications for the average stalker who, on a typical day, may have to travel some distance to where he intends to stalk. It is likely that an early start will involve some preparation the night before. There is a temptation to take the rifle and ammunition out of their usual secure place and put them ready with other equipment. Our advice is to leave such items, together with other valuables, locked away until the last moment. Many burglaries are committed whilst the occupants are asleep, totally unaware of what is occurring.

If you have a long journey, be careful if you stop for refreshments at roadside services or hotels. The fitting of security devices in vehicles specifically for firearms is not a legal requirement, but you are nevertheless responsible for the safe-keeping of both firearms and ammunition and should they be stolen from your vehicle you would have to show that all reasonable steps had been taken to prevent theft. If possible, park your vehicle where you have sight of it during your break. You should also remove the bolt and ammunition and keep them in your possession. The rifle should be locked away out of sight in the boot – this may not be possible in a four-wheel drive vehicle, so cover it up.

There are a number of excellent devices on the market for securing weapons out of sight or in the boot of your vehicle. These offer a reasonable level of security but should not be viewed as totally satisfactory, as the vehicle itself may be stolen. A good alarm system to the vehicle is a deterrent and would certainly help keep your firearm safe. In circumstances where the vehicle is to be left for a prolonged period or overnight you must take the rifle with you, secure in its slip, and make alternative arrangements for its safe-keeping. Whatever arrangements you make, it is prudent to ensure that you keep the bolt and ammunition separate from the rifle if this is possible. Additionally, make sure that when you leave your vehicle, you lock away in the boot other valuable items such as binoculars or telescopes. Knives should not be carried about in public and should also be locked away out of sight. See chapter 7.

It is impossible to lay down hard and fast rules on security when you are away from home; individual circumstances dictate varying degrees of security. Should a problem arise, matters will be judged on whether you have taken reasonable measures in the circumstances.

You should remember, too, that the legal definition of 'possession' of firearms may extend beyond actual physical possession, as we saw earlier.

Security makes sense if you value your stalking equipment and future credibility. Whilst you may never be able to deter a determined thief, there is much that can be done to prevent this type of crime and fulfil your legal obligations.

FIREARM RELATED OFFENCES

The carrying of firearms in public places

Under section 19, Firearms Act, 1968 (England, Wales and Scotland), and article 20(1), Firearms (Northern Ireland) Order, 1991, it is an offence 'without lawful authority or reasonable excuse' to have a loaded shotgun or loaded air weapon or 'any other firearm, loaded or not', together with suitable ammunition for that firearm, in a public place.

A firearm is deemed to be loaded if ammunition is in either the chamber, or the magazine from where it is capable of being fed into the chamber. A 'public place' is defined as including any highway and any other premises or place to which at the material time the public have or are permitted to have access, whether on payment or otherwise.

It is important to note that this offence could apply to a stalker's rifle, whether loaded or not – e.g. if the rifle were in your vehicle and your ammunition were separate in a box or pouch. This is not an absolute offence, however, and if it could be shown that you had either lawful authority or reasonable excuse, such as dealing with an injured deer at the roadside or possession whilst travelling to your stalking area, there is no offence. So if your possession in a public place is questioned, the emphasis should be placed on whether you have lawful authority or reasonable excuse rather than whether the rifle is in a loaded state or not. Clearly, if it is in a loaded state you will have to explain why this is necessary, and this will form the basis of your reasonable excuse. In circumstances where you are travelling by vehicle to or from stalking areas, your rifle should be unloaded with the bolt open or removed.

It is not essential to establish that a person was actually carrying a firearm provided there is a close physical link with and immediate control of it. In cases involving shotguns it is not necessary to prove that the person knew the weapon was loaded.[79]

Discharging firearms near highways etc.

England and Wales
Section 161, Highways Act, 1980, states:

> It is an offence without lawful authority or excuse to discharge any firearm within 50 feet of the centre of the highway and in consequence of which a user of the highway is injured, interrupted or endangered.

79. R v. Harrison (1995) 1 Cr. App. R. 138.

This is not an absolute offence and requires an element of complaint from a road user – a walker, rider or motorist. Provided you do not injure, interrupt or endanger someone on the highway you are entitled to shoot adjacent to it.

The sudden shot of a high-calibre rifle close to a passing horse could have serious consequences for the safety of the rider, and your suitability to be entrusted with a rifle may be also questioned. In addition you may find yourself having to defend a civil claim for damages. You should be mindful of the liabilities when considering the positioning of high seats near to highways. See chapter 7.

For this purpose a highway is a public road for vehicles. It is not an offence to shoot from or over a public footpath or right of way, or near buildings, unless you are found to be trespassing or are there with intent to endanger life.

Scotland

In Scotland it is a crime at Common Law to discharge a firearm anywhere in a culpable and reckless manner, even though no actual injury may be caused. The essence of this crime is the wanton disregard for the safety of others.

The case of Cameron v. Maguire 1998[80] is of interest to stalkers. The appellant had been convicted for recklessly discharging a loaded rifle in the direction of open woodland, to the danger of the lieges in the Isle of Mull. He had fired up to ten times from the yard of his house at a target in front of a high bank of earth which was about a foot from an open pathway leading into the woodland area, which was not obstructed by the bank. He argued that the Crown had not satisfied the test of recklessness which required there to be an utter disregard of the consequences of the act insofar as the public were concerned.[81]

The appeal was refused. It was held that the test of recklessness had been satisfied as the appellant had been firing a high-calibre rifle with a range of 3 miles, where there was a clear risk the bullet would miss the target and stray to the public footpath into the woodland area. Further to this the accuracy of the rifle was not known to the appellant as it was new and there was a risk of ricochet in the vicinity of houses and a public road. It was observed that the decision would have been the same even with the houses and public road disregarded.

80. 1999 S.C.C.R. 44.
81. Quinn v. Cunningham 1956 S.L.T. 55 (1956).

Northern Ireland
Section 20(2), the Firearms (Northern Ireland) Order, 1981, provides that a person who discharges any firearm on any public road, or within 60 feet of the centre of any road, or in any street, passage of a town, church, churchyard or burial ground shall be guilty of an offence unless they establish to the satisfaction of the court that they did it for a purpose that was reasonable and lawful.

Shooting from vehicles

In the absence of case law on this subject it is our opinion that the offences below relate to shooting from within a vehicle rather than the situation where the stalker is outside the stationary vehicle and using part of the bodywork as a 'lean' when taking the shot.

England, Wales and Northern Ireland
Under section 4(4), Deer Act, 1991, and article 19(3)(b), Wildlife (Northern Ireland) Order, 1981, it is an offence to shoot at deer from a mechanically propelled vehicle unless on enclosed land where deer are usually kept. A vehicle would include an aircraft or boat.[82]

Scotland
Under section 20, Deer (Scotland) Act, 1996, it is an offence to shoot at deer from any *moving* vehicle, unless it is to prevent the suffering of an injured or diseased deer or calf about to be deprived of its mother. An exemption exists under section 41(2) for the taking of deer (alive) in any manner provided it does not cause unnecessary suffering.

The law differs from that in England, Wales and Northern Ireland in that shooting from a stationary vehicle is not prohibited. But shooting from a stationary vehicle away from the highway has inherent dangers. Extra care is required to ensure the safety of the participants and the humane dispatch of the deer. In Scotland such shooting can take place at night under authorisation from the Deer Commission for the purposes of crop protection. The Code of Practice for Night Shooting should be strictly adhered to.[83]

The Act also restricts the driving of deer by vehicle on any land, for the purposes of taking or killing them, to those people with written authorisation from the Deer Commission. The Code of Practice on the Use of Vehicles for the Purposes of Deer Management issued by the Commission should be followed.[84]

82. See chapter 2.
83. See page 55–58.
84. See page 52–54.

Trespassing with firearms

Under section 20(1) and (2), Firearms Act, 1968, it is an offence for a person to enter or be upon any land (including water) or building or part of a building as a trespasser whilst in possession of a firearm[85] without reasonable excuse. A similar offence exists in the Firearms (Northern Ireland) Order, 1981, under article 21(1) and (2), in which the proof of reasonable excuse lies on the accused.

As to whether following up a wounded beast would be considered a reasonable excuse would be for a court to decide. The aggrieved party might view the explanation as a cover for the poaching of deer. The criminal and civil liabilities of crossing your boundary in these circumstances are dealt with in chapter 7.

It is also worth noting that under section 21(5) of the Deer (Scotland) Act, 1996, any person who uses any firearm or any ammunition for the purpose of wilfully injuring any deer shall be guilty of an offence.

VISITS TO AND FROM ABROAD

Visits abroad

If you wish to stalk deer abroad and take your rifle, you must ensure that you are able to comply with the requirements the country may have for visiting stalkers. If the country to be visited is another E.U. member,[86] you will need to obtain a European Firearms Pass (E.F.P.). These are obtainable without charge from the firearms licensing department of your local police force and can cover any section 1 firearm for which you have a certificate.

The E.F.P. will be valid for the duration of your current certificate, after which it can be renewed. You may also change or extend your E.F.P. to cover other firearms. Permission or authorisation from the authorities of the country to be visited should be obtained prior to your visit and put on your E.F.P. However, this is not normally required from an E.U. country if you are using the firearms for stalking, hunting or marksmanship activities. Certain categories of firearms, however, are prohibited by some states. These are laid down in the E.C. Directive on the Control of the Acquisition and Possession of Weapons, 91/477/E.E.C.

---

85. This means any firearm, including an air weapon.
86. Austria, Belgium, Denmark, Finland, France, Germany, Greece, the Republic of Ireland, Italy, Luxembourg, Netherlands, Portugal, Spain and Sweden.

During your visit you must carry your E.F.P. whenever you have your rifle with you. You should be able to prove the reason for your trip and must produce your E.F.P. to the police or customs officers if requested.

An information leaflet entitled *The European Firearms Pass* is produced by the Home Departments and is normally available from your local police licensing department.

Visits to Northern Ireland

Stalkers wishing to take a rifle to Northern Ireland must first obtain a certificate of approval from the Royal Ulster Constabulary, Firearms Licensing Branch, Linasharragh, Montgomery Road, Belfast. There is no fee. Visiting stalkers are required to specify details of their firearms certificate and stalking arrangements whilst in the country. Applications must be made well in advance of your visit (at least a month). A copy of your firearm certificate must be sent with the application, together with a letter of permission or authority to stalk.

Firearms may be imported to Northern Ireland by a person normally resident outside the U.K. provided that either a Northern Ireland visitor's firearm certificate or a Northern Ireland three-year firearm certificate has been issued by the Chief Constable of the Royal Ulster Constabulary. Application must be made not less than two months before the proposed date of arrival. There is no fee payable for the visitor's firearm certificate.

Application forms together with other information that may be required, are obtainable from Royal Ulster Constabulary, Firearms Licensing Department, Knocknagoney House, Knocknagoney Road, Belfast BT4 2PP.

Visits to the Republic of Ireland

Over 3000 overseas shooters visit Ireland each year, many of them for the purpose of deer stalking. The Republic has separate licensing arrangements and being a member of the E.U., visitors must first obtain an E.F.P., as described above. Deer stalkers should note that

123

centre-fire calibres greater than .22 (5.56 mm) are prohibited and therefore they must first obtain a visitor's firearm certificate if they wish to take or use their own rifle. The minimum calibres for shooting deer are .22–250 centre-fire and the maximum is .270.

Application forms for firearms certificates can be obtained from the Department of Justice, Firearms Section, 72–76 St Stephens Green, Dublin. Certificates are granted on the basis of the issue of a hunting licence, for which there is no charge. This is obtainable from the Wildlife Service, Leeson Lane, Dublin. The licence must be forwarded with your application for the firearm certificate. It is stressed that applications should be made well in advance – at least a month before your visit.

Visits to Great Britain

The provisions for visitors are contained in the Firearms (Amendment) Act, 1988. Under section 17, all visitors who want to bring a firearm into Great Britain or possess one here must first obtain a visitor's firearm permit. The application for such permits must be made on the applicant's behalf by a sponsor or representative, to the chief officer of police for the area in which he lives. Application forms are available from police stations or the local licensing department. The sponsor or representative may be acting in a private capacity, or may be a professional stalker or an official or employee of a shooting organisation or agency. He does not necessarily need to have a firearm certificate himself. An information leaflet, *Permits for Visitors to Great Britain* is published by the Home Departments and is normally available from police licensing departments.

Section 18 of the Act provides that a permit is not required for the purchase of a firearm if it is exported without it coming into the visitor's possession in this country. You may only do this if you have not been in Great Britain for more than thirty days in the preceding twelve months. Additionally a permit is not required where an estate rifle is used by the visitor.[87]

Under E.U. Directive 91/477/E.E.C. there are special require-ments for visitors from other E.U. states. In addition to the British visitor's permit they must also possess an E.F.P. issued by the auth-orities of their country of residence. When a sponsor or representative applies for a British visitor's permit the E.F.P. must be sent with the application to the chief officer of police. Both permits must be with the visitor when bringing the firearm into the country and at all times

87. See page 108.

when he is in possession of the firearm whilst here. They must be produced to a police or customs officer on demand.

The import and export of firearms

The import and export of firearms and ammunition are controlled in Great Britain and appropriate licences must be obtained from the Department of Trade and Industry (D.T.I.). The E.C. Weapons Directive (91/477/E.E.C.) applies only to movements of firearms between member states; other countries are subject to normal licensing procedures.

For commercial importations, D.T.I. import licenses are only issued to importers authorised by the police as registered firearms dealers. Open individual licenses may be issued for non-prohibited section 1 firearms and ammunition, or, in the case of an importation from another E.U. member state, a transfer licence issued by the member state.

As an extra statutory concession, certain firearms which are covered by a valid section 1 firearm certificate or a British visitor's firearms permit may be accepted in lieu of an import licence for the non-commercial importation of a section 1 firearm. If the firearm is being imported from another E.U. country, the importer must also hold an E.F.P. detailing the firearm being imported.

An export licence is not required if you are taking your rifle to another E.U. member state as part of your personal effects for a stalking holiday or competition, provided an E.F.P. is held and the firearm is not one of a restricted class. You cannot use your E.F.P. if you intend taking the rifle there on a permanent basis. To do this you will need a licence from the D.T.I.

You can obtain more information and advice about the licensing requirements from the Export Licensing Unit, Department of Trade and Industry, Kingsgate House, 66–74 Victoria Street, London SW1E 6SW. If you require more advice about the E.F.P., taking firearms abroad or buying firearms in other E.U. states, you should contact the firearms licensing department of your local police.

CHAPTER 7

Stalking Liabilities

As you travel to your stalking ground it is doubtful whether your thoughts will be on your responsibility to comply with the law. You are more likely to be thinking of the weather, the direction of the wind and conditions underfoot, which will ultimately dictate your stalking tactics. You may have a knife at your side and a high-calibre rifle with ammunition in the vehicle, yet as a prudent stalker with honest intentions you should pose no threat to public safety or the environment – unlike the 38-ton articulated lorry that has just overtaken you in the fast lane!

But whether you are stalking alone or as a guest, you must ensure that you do not contravene the law or put at risk your own or the public's safety. This can only be achieved with proper training and by having a thorough knowledge of the law. Minimising liabilities particularly in potentially dangerous situations should be everyone's aim.

RESPONSIBLE DEER MANAGEMENT

Whilst there is no substitute for hands-on experience gained over time and under the direct supervision of an experienced stalker, formal training courses are available that lay the foundations for safe and responsible stalking. Indeed, such qualifications may in the future be essential in assessing an individual's suitability to cull deer with a rifle.[88]

A progressive system of deer management qualifications relevant to both professional and recreational deer managers and stalkers has now been developed. Known as the Deer Stalking Certificate, its aim is to set standards of competence for the efficient and humane culling of deer in line with the government's vocational qualifications. The new certificate is awarded by Deer Management Qualifications Limited (D.M.Q.),[89] a company set up by participating organisations from within the industry to develop, set and monitor the standards for wild deer management. Both the B.A.S.C. and the B.D.S. are assessment centres for this purpose.

A number of deer management courses are available including a B.D.S. Advanced Stalker's Course and a Forestry Commission Deer Management Course.

Once a stalker has gained the appropriate qualifications, or gained experience privately, there are a number of other requirements that should be satisfied prior to stalking.

Legal requirements relating to firearms

You should hold an appropriate firearm certificate covering both the weapon and ammunition. Your intended use of the weapon and ammunition must comply with the conditions of your certificate.[90] Of particular importance is the safe-keeping condition.

Game licences

If you are shooting on 'unenclosed' land, you must have a licence to kill game. This requirement may appear somewhat confusing, since deer are not classed as 'game'.[91] But section 4 of the Game Licences Act, 1860, states that such a licence is required by anyone who takes, kills or pursues, or assists in doing so, any game, woodcock, snipe, rabbit or *deer* on unenclosed land. Section 5 provides an exemption for pursuing and killing deer by hunting with hounds (which is legal in England and Wales only), or the taking and killing of deer in enclosed lands by the owner or occupier or by those under his

88. See chapter 6.
89. See page 205 for contact details.
90. See chapter 6.
91. See chapter 1.

127

direction or permission. 'Enclosed land' means land used for farming and enclosed by normal agricultural hedges; in our view this would include fenced forestry blocks.[92] However, on moorland, for example, a licence would be required. There has been speculation about the possible abolition of the licence, but it has not yet been included in any deregulation Act and it remains a legal requirement.

Authority to be on the land

You may own the land or the sporting rights to the deer, in which case the authority is clear. Where this is not the case you may simply have verbal authority from the owner or occupier of the land. This is sufficient, provided he has a right to give such permission. Should the stalking rights be let[93] then such authority would need to be given by the holder of the rights.

Our advice is that all such authorities should ideally be in writing and should specify what you can and cannot shoot. Oral permission is a recipe for uncertainty and should anything go wrong the landowner could deny he gave you permission. We have assisted some major landowners in formulating their own firearms policy, and we advise that it should include guidance and the issuing of authorities to be on land with firearms. An identification system can be incorporated into the policy, in which users of section 1 firearms are issued with a personal document providing details of their authority. This can provide assurance to police and members of the public should the holder be challenged. It may also help prevent breaches of the law relating to armed trespass and poaching.

Knowledge of the land to be stalked

A good knowledge of the land is essential not only for safe shooting but also for efficient deer management. You should have an awareness of where footpaths and highways dissect the land, and knowledge of other sporting or farming activities. This information may make a difference to when and where you stalk. You should also have a clear understanding of where the boundaries lie. This is essential as ignorance will be a poor defence should you be found trespassing with a firearm. A number of liabilities arise in such situations and are elaborated upon on page 132.

---

92. Jemmison v. Priddle 1971. See page 134.
93. See chapter 1.

Making the landowner or occupier aware of your presence

This may not always be practical or useful in remote, isolated areas which are owned by absentee landlords. But in other areas arrangements should be made in advance where possible and the owner notified of your visit. Alternatively, some form of notice should be given from which it can easily be ascertained that you are stalking, such as a fax message, an advance list of dates, displaying red flags (often used on the open hill).

Identification of quarry

Even experienced stalkers can make a mistake in identification but the occasions should be rare and the error corrected before the trigger is squeezed. Mistaken identification may be grounds for mitigation but is no defence in law. The liabilities involved depend on whether what has been shot by mistake is protected at the time by close season.

Mistakes are more likely to be made in identifying the sexes rather than the species – an error in identifying the latter would be unforgivable. Care is required when shooting roe deer at the time when the bucks are casting antlers and in their close season. Time should be taken to ensure the correct sexing of immature deer that may not be showing obvious signs of antler development.

Stalker training and qualifications take account of the importance of identification but there is no substitute for experience in the field. As Ken Macarthur, the great roe expert in Scotland would say, 'Time has to be spent watching deer – without the rifle!'

The following sketches may be of assistance.

Red   Fallow   Sika   Roe   Muntjac   Chinese Water

FALLOW DEER

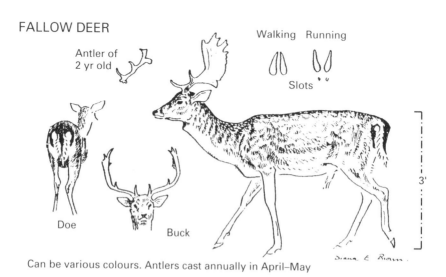

Antler of 2 yr old

Walking   Running

Slots

Doe

Buck

3'

Can be various colours. Antlers cast annually in April–May

RED DEER

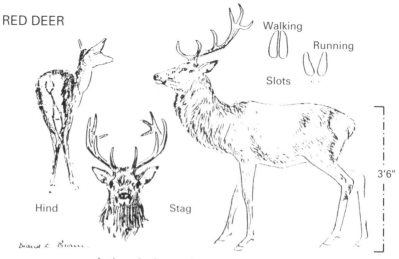

Walking

Running

Slots

Hind

Stag

3'6"

Antlers shed annually about March

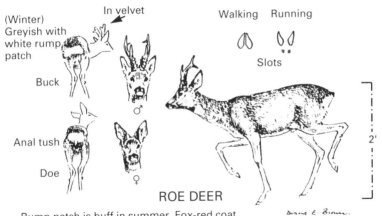

(Winter)
Greyish with
white rump
patch

In velvet

Walking   Running

Slots

Buck

♂

Anal tush

Doe

♀

ROE DEER

Rump patch is buff in summer. Fox-red coat.
Antlers cast annually in November–December

2'

Diana E. Brown.

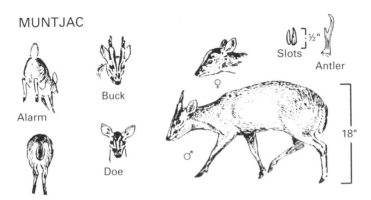

MUNTJAC

Alarm

Buck

Doe

♀

♂

Slots   ½"

Antler

18"

Dark glossy brown – chestnut flanks

Diana E. Brown

SIKA DEER

Hind

Stag

2"+

Alarmed

2'9"

Winter – Grey/brown – stags can appear black. Head greyish
Summer – Dappled chestnut. Head greyish

Antlers cast annually in March–May

Diana E. Brown

STALKING NEAR BOUNDARIES

One essential task prior to stalking any new ground is to gain a thorough knowledge of exactly where boundaries lie. If you have doubts you may become preoccupied when your full concentration should be on the job in hand. You should not be relying on the adjacent landowner, tenant or stalker to tell you that you have got it wrong. This is embarrassing and unprofessional – and not without liability. Clarification of boundaries can be an onerous task and in some cases may lead to disputes, but it must be set against the liabilities involved in ignoring them and the advantages it may bring. You should try and obtain a plan or large-scale ordinance survey map on which you can clearly mark boundaries once you have clarified them with the owner. On new ground you should ensure that you walk the boundaries, without your rifle and with the owner if this is possible.

Civil action for simple trespass may be taken by a landowner against anyone setting foot on his land without permission[94] (although in Scotland it is necessary to show that damage has occurred). If you are found on the wrong side of the fence you may be sued for damages in the civil court, although unless substantial damage or nuisance can be shown, any damages are likely to be minimal. However, if you are carrying your rifle at the time, loaded or not, and have no reasonable excuse, you may be prosecuted for the criminal offence of trespass with a firearm.[95] Where persistent trespass takes place an injunction may also be applied for to prevent further infringements.

Trespass is not confined to your own physical entry onto another's property but could extend to sending your dog or firing a shot over the boundary.

Shooting deer close to your boundary will inevitably lead to the dilemma of a shot beast running over the line before falling dead or continuing with an injury. For the responsible stalker this situation should not present a problem as agreements will previously have been made with the adjacent landowner or tenant to cater for this type of occurrence. The beast will be retrieved or followed up and a courtesy call made to inform the neighbour of the incident.

Where such amicable arrangements have not been or cannot be made then to retrieve the beast or go in search of it without first obtaining permission will incur liabilities. Claims over the ownership of a carcase, where boundaries are in dispute, can be difficult to assess and ultimately would have to be decided by a court. However the

94. See chapter 8.
95. See chapter 6.

Common Law principle is that property in a wild animal, should it fall dead, is vested in the owner of the land where it has died.

You may well consider you have a claim of ownership of the beast,[96] but in entering the land without permission you commit an act of trespass and have no legal right to be there, even if you are following up an injured animal. You may have to defend yourself against an allegation of trespassing with a firearm (contrary to section 20 of the Firearms Act, 1968), and you would have to convince the court that in pursuing the injured beast you had a reasonable excuse. At the very least an action could lie against you for simple trespass to land (England and Wales only). The obvious suspicion will be that you are a poacher and shot the deer over the boundary.

Liability may not be confined to the civil courts since the legislation protecting deer caters for offences of removing a carcase from land.[97] Although this legislation is designed to combat poachers returning to the land having killed deer the previous night, it may come into effect when a stalker's behaviour is suspicious and warrants legal action – e.g. when deer are being discreetly shot over a boundary and then retrieved on the excuse that they were legitimately shot but then crossed the boundary before falling dead.

We do not consider that proceedings are appropriate for the offence of removing a carcase from land if there is genuine evidence that the beast shot was legitimately on land where authority existed. In such cases careful examination of the area where the beast was shot should

96. See chapter 1.
97. See chapters 2 and 3.

be made in an attempt to reveal blood and hair (paint and pins) which may corroborate the evidence.

The case of Jemmison v. Priddle, 1971, involved the shooting of deer close to a boundary. One of the deer, a red hind, was shot on land where permission had been granted. The animal subsequently ran and dropped dead on the other side of the boundary. Although the case centred on whether the land was 'enclosed' for the purpose of exemption from the need for a game licence (elaborated upon above) it was accepted that deer shot legitimately on land where permission was granted may run and drop on land where no such permission existed. However, the case did not rule on the rights of ownership of the deer in question, which was seized by the owner of the land where it fell.

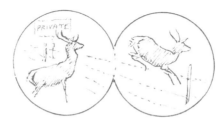

When there are disputes over where boundaries lie, there is a need to minimise the liabilities involved. Most situations are preventable, particularly if you resist pulling the trigger and wait for a better opportunity on another beast that is not so close to the boundary. Alternatively, it may be a case for getting in close and taking a neck shot, thereby preventing movement after the shot has been taken. Constructive trespass can also occur where your bullet travels on over the land where you do not have permission to shoot.[98] Liaison with neighbours is a matter of common courtesy and often mutually beneficial agreements can be achieved.

THE SHOOTING OF NON-TARGET SPECIES

Opportunities occasionally present themselves for the stalker to shoot non-protected species other than deer; wild goats, boar and foxes spring to mind. Authority for the shooting of other species should be obtained from the owner of the land (or the shooting rights). The firearm certificate for your stalking rifle should cater for such a

98. See chapter 8.

variation, i.e. that the conditions of use include wild goat, boar or fox control. The term 'vermin' may cover wild boar and foxes but you should clarify this with the licensing department of the issuing police force. If your certificate has been granted on the basis of deer stalking only, that is all you are legally entitled to shoot and therefore to shoot something other than a deer, irrespective of the circumstances, will render you liable for a breach of certificate conditions. These conditions are important, and you should be fully aware of exactly what is written there. Remember, you are at risk of revocation if you breach the conditions.[99]

Wild boar

Wild boar are a former native species of Britain but became extinct in the seventeenth century. The farming of wild boar has now become popular and a considerable number are reared for their meat. The British Wild Boar Association (B.W.B.A.) was founded to promote wild boar farming and membership is voluntary.[100] The Association has been actively involved in consultations with the Ministry of Agriculture, Fisheries and Food (M.A.F.F.) and other interested bodies on the current status and impact of wild boar escapees.

It has now been confirmed by the M.A.F.F. that a number of free-living wild boar exist in some southern counties of England. There is evidence that the animals, which are thought to have escaped originally from farm enclosures, are breeding in the wild. The boar are not marked or tagged to signify ownership and, since they are free to roam where they please and are thought to be reproducing, they are considered as wild – *ferae naturae*.

99. See chapter 6.
100. See page 204 for contact details.

Wild boar may only be kept under licence issued by local authorities, either under the Dangerous Wild Animals Act, 1976, in the case of private keepers or under the Zoo Licensing Act, 1981, for collections open to the public. With the exception of the Wildlife and Countryside Act, 1981, which prohibits their release or escape into the wild, no legislation exists which affords any protection for the species once they become wild. Where they have established themselves in the wild they may therefore be killed or taken by owners and occupiers of land or persons with their authority using any method, including shooting. The B.A.S.C. advises that any of the sporting rifles which can be used against the larger species of British deer – sika, fallow and red – would be suitable for boar and recommend .270 calibre or larger, with suitable ammunition. The B.W.B.A. has issued guidance on dealing with escapee boar.

Liabilities arise if wild boar are shot which are identifiable as captive in areas close to wild boar farms, where temporary escapes may be expected. In this situation the boar may be classed as property in the same way as straying livestock. The owner may attempt either to make a civil claim against the shooter for damages and return of the carcase or to report the matter to the police, who would consider whether criminal damage had been committed.[101]

No case law exists on wild boar and therefore their status has not been determined. In the absence of such a determination they might reasonably be considered to be vermin, given its current Oxford Dictionary definition of 'mammals or birds injurious to game, crops etc.'. This interpretation has important implications for deer stalkers who use expanding ammunition, the use of which is restricted by the provisions of sections 9 and 10 of the Firearms (Amendment) Act, 1997. Section 10(b)(ii) provides that expanding ammunition may be used for 'the shooting of vermin or, in the course of carrying on activities with the management of any estate, other wildlife'. It is reasonable to assume therefore, in the absence of a legal ruling, that wild boar could fall within either exemption and therefore be shot by a stalker using expanding ammunition. As we have said, this of course assumes that the appropriate condition exists on his firearm certificate – i.e. culling of wild boar or vermin. Our advice would be for the former condition to be sought rather than rely on the description of vermin.

It is uncertain what if any protection will be afforded wild boar in the future. They could be regarded as a native species with a biodiversity and sporting value, or conversely as an invasive pest.

---

101. See chapter 1 on theft of and criminal damage to escaped captive animals.

CRUELTY AND HUMANE DISPATCH

Historically the law has not protected wild animals such as deer from acts of cruelty. Only in situations where wild deer could be considered as captive have they come within the legislation protecting animals against acts of cruelty. The provisions of the Protection of Animals Act, 1911, or the Protection of Animals (Scotland) Act, 1912, only provide protection for animals that are defined as 'domestic or captive'.[102] There may be circumstances in which wild deer may be deemed to be 'captive' and therefore the stalker needs to be aware of the liabilities involved.

In addition, the Welfare of Animals Act (Northern Ireland), 1972, and the Wild Mammals Protection Act, 1996, now provide protection in certain circumstances for deer in their wild state against acts of cruelty. See page 141.

The Protection of Animals Acts

The Protection of Animals Act, 1911, and the Protection of Animals (Scotland) Act, 1912, define a captive animal as 'any animal . . . which is in captivity, or confinement, or which is maimed, pinioned, or subjected to any appliance or contrivance for the purpose of hindering or preventing its escape'.

The Acts create offences of cruelly beating, kicking, ill-treating, over-riding, over-driving, torturing, infuriating or terrifying any animal, or causing the animal any unnecessary suffering by wantonly or unreasonably doing or omitting to do any act.

Two past cases, both considered by the Court of Appeal, involved allegations of cruelty to deer and are relevant in determining the circumstances in which deer may be viewed by the courts as being in captivity or a state of confinement.

The first of these is Rogers v. Pickersgill, 1910. At the time of this case it was a matter of great controversy as to whether the hunting of semi-captive animals should be allowed at all. An exception existed at the time (and still does under section 1(3)(b)) for the coursing or hunting of any captive animal, unless such animal is liberated in an injured, mutilated or exhausted condition. In addition the exception would not apply if the animal at the time was still in captivity, or had been recaptured or brought under control. The legislation catered here, amongst other hunting and coursing practices, for the hunting of 'carted' deer.[103]

102. The effect of these Acts in relation to farmed or wild deer kept in captivity are dealt with in detail in chapter 1.
103. See page 15 for a description of 'carted' deer.

The circumstances of the case were that a hind (previously released from a cart) was being hunted by hounds and twice took refuge in a yard, where it backed into a shed. It was poked and whipped to get it out. The hounds again gave chase. Eventually, after colliding with a barbed wire fence, by which it was injured, it was dragged in a state of exhaustion along a road, where it fell down and died.

The Master of Hounds was subsequently summoned to court for an offence of cruelty to the hind while *in captivity*. The case centred on whether, at the point when the hind had backed into the shed, the hunt was over and, if that was the case, the exemption under the above section did not apply. The magistrates initially dismissed the case on the basis that the acts were done at a time when the hunt was not at an end and during the course of the hunting of the animal, and therefore fell within the legal exemption.

Following an appeal it was apparent that the magistrates had not heard all the evidence. Hence the case as stated did not rule on whether cruelty offences were committed or whether the hunt had ended. The judge was sufficiently satisfied that there was at least a *prima facie* case that what was done was done when the hunt was finished and therefore the case was remitted to the magistrate's court to hear evidence in answer to the facts proved.

The appeal court were of the opinion that hunting involved pursuit, and once an animal had taken refuge from being pursued any cruelty that was committed upon it may not be excused on the grounds that the hunt was still continuing (and therefore exempt).

The second case was Rowley v. Murphy, 1963. The circumstances of this case involved hunting a wild stag with hounds. The stag jumped over the hedge of a field onto a main road, slipped on the tarmac surface and went under a stationary van. The stag was dragged from beneath the van and carried into an enclosure nearby, where it was killed with a knife.

The Master of Hounds was summoned to court for the offence of cruelly terrifying an animal by cutting its throat with a knife, contrary to section 1(1)(a) of the Protection of Animals Act, 1911. The justices found that there was no case to answer on the basis that the stag was not an 'animal' within the meaning of the Act, i.e. not in captivity or confinement at the time of the incident. On appeal by the prosecutor it was contended that there was a case to answer and the case centred on whether the hunted stag at the point of killing was captive or in confinement. It was not of concern to the court whether what was done was cruel or not. The sole question was whether the stag in all the circumstances came within the scope of the legislation – i.e. was the animal in a state of captivity or confinement at the time the alleged cruelty was committed.

The court took due regard of the history of the legislation and a number of previous cases were referred to during the case, in particular Steele v. Rogers, 1912, in which it was stated that a mere temporary inability to get away was not a 'state of captivity' and that something more than mere captivity was necessary, such as some period of time during which 'acts of dominion' are exercised over the animal before it can be said to be in a state of captivity.

Judgement was made between whether 'captivity' starts the moment an animal is captured and hands are laid on the animal and prevented from escaping, or whether the words 'in captivity' denote a state of affairs in which domination is exercised over the animal beyond mere capture. In referring to the exemption for hunting and coursing of any 'captive' animal it was noted that *recapture* brings an animal into a state of 'captivity'. A clear distinction was drawn between 'in captivity' meaning a state of captivity and that of an animal being captive, i.e. subject temporarily to restraint by human beings.

It was subsequently held that a mere temporary inability to get away was not a state of captivity, and the words 'captive animal' meant by definition an animal in captivity or confinement, so the stag was not an animal within the meaning or protection of the Act. The appeal was dismissed.

Humane dispatch

There may be circumstances in which a stalker will have to dispatch deer that may be considered as 'captive' at the time by virtue of the fact that it is wounded and is prevented from escaping. Therefore the stalker's actions must not cause unnecessary suffering. Training in and experience of humane dispatch are therefore essential.

In a stalking situation a wounded beast should be dispatched with the rifle from a safe distance. There may be exceptional circumstances where this may not be possible or practical, in which case a knife can be used provided it is done in such a manner that it does not cause unnecessary suffering to the beast. It should be done in a swift and humane manner, which requires adequate training and experience on the part of the stalker, who should adhere to accepted practice and guidance given by such bodies as the British Deer Society and the B.A.S.C.[104] It is stressed that this should only be necessary in exceptional circumstances.

If a complaint is made against a stalker for the manner in which he

---

104. An advice note is available from the B.A.S.C.

has dispatched an injured deer, consideration would be given to whether a cruelty offence (Protection of Animals Act, 1911, Protection of Animals (Scotland) Act, 1912) had been committed. The first consideration would be whether in the circumstances the beast was captive or in a state of captivity, as discussed above. If this were the case and the actions of the stalker were considered to be unnecessary, matters could proceed to court. Two questions arise in establishing whether the act complained of was necessary and done with the minimum of suffering: what did the stalker do – e.g. cut the beast's throat with a sharp, suitable knife – and what was the reason for doing it – e.g. to prevent further suffering. If the reason is sufficiently important to justify the act, even if it is bodged through inexperience, then we do not consider an offence would be committed.

We are of the opinion that in normal stalking conditions, carrying handguns solely in case one needs to dispatch injured deer is neither practical nor necessary.[105] There is a case for some individuals, such as rangers and deer managers, who are regularly called out to deal with injured deer, often road casualties, to be licensed for the use of suitable handguns[106] or other slaughtering instruments for dispatching deer at close quarters. As explained in chapter 6, any shotgun can be used in this situation but not a rifle below the minimum calibre permitted under the Deer Acts. This restriction has been unwittingly abused by the use of the .22 rim-fire rifle which is considered by many to be more appropriate and perfectly adequate to dispatch deer in these circumstances. It is, however, illegal.

It is worth noting that section 6(2), Deer Act, 1991, section 25 Deer (Scotland) Act, 1996, and article 20 The Wildlife (Northern Ireland) Order, 1985[107] provide legal exemptions against certain acts done for the purpose of preventing suffering of injured or diseased deer. It is stressed that these exemptions relate only to acts done that would otherwise be offences as specified within the Deer Acts. They do not exempt any act that may incur liabilities under other legislation. For example, shooting a deer during the close season is an offence but if done to prevent suffering no offence would be committed under the Deer Acts. However if a firearm was used in breach of the certificate conditions, for whatever purpose, an offence under the Firearms Act would be committed.

---

105. See chapter 6.
106. A single-shot .32 handgun is recommended by the R.S.P.C.A.
107. See chapters 2 and 3.

The Welfare of Animals Act (Northern Ireland), 1972

Sections 13 and 14 in Part III of the Act relate to offences of cruelty to any animal and are similar to the equivalent legislation in England, Wales and Scotland in describing the acts that will constitute cruelty offences. The key difference is that the legislation is not restricted to animals described as 'captive or domestic'. Hence any animal, wild or otherwise is included.

Section 15 provides for a number of exemptions to the offences of cruelty which may be of relevance to stalkers:

- acts done in the course of, or in the preparation for, the destruction of any animal as food for human consumption, unless unnecessary suffering is caused to the animal
- acts done in the course of the hunting, pursuit, coursing, capture or destruction of any wild animal, unless unnecessary suffering is caused to the animal
- the coursing or hunting of any animal, other than a domestic animal, which is released for that purpose and which is not under control, unless it was released in an injured, mutilated or exhausted condition

The Wild Mammals (Protection) Act, 1996

This Act, covering England, Wales and Scotland, represents the first legislation to protect all wild mammals from certain acts of cruelty. Pressure for its introduction was brought to bear on the government following a number of well-publicised cases of cruelty to wild animals, in situations where legal action was not possible against the offenders, e.g. the kicking to death of a hedgehog.

Section 1 provides that if any person mutilates, kicks, beats, nails or otherwise impales, stabs, burns, stones, crushes, drowns, drags or asphyxiates any wild animal (as defined below) with intent to inflict unnecessary suffering, he shall be guilty of an offence.

Section 2 gives certain exemptions:

A person shall not be guilty of an offence by reason of:

(a) the attempted killing of a wild mammal as an act of mercy if he shows that the mammal had been so seriously disabled otherwise than by his unlawful act and that there was no reasonable chance of its recovering;
(b) the killing in a reasonably swift and humane manner of any wild animal if he shows that the mammal had been injured or taken in

141

the course of either lawful shooting, hunting, coursing or pest control activity;

(c)   doing anything which is authorised by or under any enactment;

(d)   any act made unlawful by section 1 if the act was done by means of any snare, trap, dog, or bird lawfully used for the purpose of killing or taking any wild animal; or

(e)   the lawful use of any poisonous or noxious substance on any wild mammal.

The Act defines 'wild mammal' as any mammal which is not domestic or captive within the meaning of the Protection of Animals Act, 1911, or the Protection of Animals (Scotland) Act, 1912.

The exemptions listed at (a) and (b) are clearly relevant to the dispatch of injured deer. The key issues for the stalker are:

• The deer must not have been injured by the stalker's unlawful acts. A poacher would therefore not be able to claim this legal exemption in respect of a deer injured by him, but someone innocently coming across a deer in the road who attempted to put it out of its misery but bodged the killing through inexperience would not commit an offence under this Act.

• Such dispatch should be reasonably swift and humane and the deer must have been injured or taken by lawful shooting etc. This exemption emphasises the point that the dispatch of deer should be done in the correct manner as described by the organisations responsible for competency qualifications.[108]

  If allegations were made that such a killing was not swift and humane it would be important in any defence for the stalker to show that his actions were in accordance with accepted practice. It should be noted that the exemption would not apply if it could be shown that the activity you were involved in was unlawful – e.g. if you were trespassing or you were in breach of the conditions of your firearm certificate.

THE CARRYING OF KNIVES

No responsible deer stalker would set out without a sharp, suitable knife. It is an essential piece of equipment, its main use being to facilitate bleeding of the carcase and the gralloch. Good stalkers pride themselves on the quality of their knives and their safe use, but few

---

108.   See page 127.

stop to consider the liabilities involved in carrying them.

The increase in knife-related crime, particularly amongst young criminals, has led to substantial legislation restricting the possession of knives. There have been periodic amnesties; the one in 1996 yielding 38,000 weapons, including many formidable knives. The problem for the legislators over the years has been in framing the law to prevent the carrying of knives, which may be used for causing injury, and at the same time allow them to be routinely carried for wholly justifiable and innocent purposes, for example by stalkers.

The following legislation shows that the emphasis is on the prevention of crime, penalising the possession of knives in public places.

The Prevention of Crime Act, 1953 (England and Wales)

It is an offence to carry an offensive weapon in a public place without lawful authority or reasonable excuse (the onus is on the defendant to prove lawful authority or excuse). The term 'offensive weapon' includes any article made, adapted or intended for causing injury to a person. 'Public place' is defined as any place to which the public have access at the material time. This includes areas where an open access policy may apply.

The Restriction of Offensive Weapons Act, 1959 and 1961 (England, Wales and Scotland)

This legislation identifies certain specific weapons, including flick knives and gravity knives, and creates offences in respect of their manufacture and sale.

The Criminal Justice Act, 1988 (England, Wales and Scotland)

This Act is similar to the 1953 Act, but Subsection 139 creates the offence of possessing, in a public place, any article which has a blade or is sharply pointed, except a folding pocket knife with a blade not exceeding 3 inches.

A defence is provided if the person can show he had good reason or lawful authority for having the article with him in a public place or had it with him for use at work, for religious reasons or as part of any national costume.

The Offensive Weapons Act, 1996 (England, Wales and Scotland)

This Act increases police powers of arrest and extended the law to cover school premises. It prohibits the sale of knives to persons under sixteen, and creates an indictable offence of carrying an offensive weapon, for which the offender can be sent for trial at the Crown Court.

Under the Act the offences described above – i.e. carrying offensive weapons such as knives without lawful authority or reasonable excuse (1953 Act) and having an article with a blade or point in a public place or school premises (1988 Act) – were made 'arrestable', giving the police (and civilians in certain circumstances) the power to make immediate arrests without warrant. The police may also arrest on suspicion.

The Knives Act, 1997 (England, Wales and Scotland)

This Act has two main objectives. The first is to create new criminal offences in relation to the possession, marketing and publishing of material about certain knives. The second is to confer powers on the police to stop and search people or vehicles for knives and other offensive weapons.

Under section 1 of the Act it is an offence to market a knife in a way that indicates or suggests that it is suitable for combat or is likely to stimulate or encourage violent behaviour involving the use of the knife as a weapon. Such a knife is described as being one 'suitable for use as a weapon for inflicting injury or causing fear, being an instrument with a blade or is sharply pointed'. Consequently any knife in the above circumstances may fall within the provisions of the Act.

The practical implications of the legislation

Whilst stalking it is unlikely that you will be in a public place and the carrying of a knife, should it ever be questioned, will be easily justified. Once in a public place – travelling in your car or visiting the local shop – the situation changes somewhat in that you may have to prove that you have a reasonable excuse or good reason for carrying your knife or, if you are a professional deer manager or ranger, that you have it for use at work.

Individual circumstances will dictate whether possession of a knife at a particular time and place can be justified. This is very much a matter of common sense, in that stalkers should be aware of the implications of carrying a knife overtly in a public place where concern or criticism may be expressed. Our advice is to remove them, if they are visible, prior to visiting places where concerns may be raised. Forgetting you are wearing a knife may not be an acceptable defence.

LIABILITIES THROUGH NEGLIGENCE OR LACK OF CARE

Stalkers

Stalking activities can be potentially hazardous and in civil law you owe a duty to others to take reasonable care so as not to cause them foreseeable injury. If you fail to exercise such care and your negligence results in injury to another person or damage to property, then you may be liable to the victim. If you are reckless then, in addition to incurring civil liabilities, you may find yourself facing a criminal prosecution.

The stalker who takes a reckless shot which results in someone being injured or killed may be liable in both criminal and civil law. If the court considered that he was grossly negligent or reckless the consequences could be serious and a criminal charge may result in a term of imprisonment. There is a considerable amount of case law and difference of opinion about the extent of culpability in such circumstances and much would depend on the circumstances of each individual case.

Shots taken with no suitable back stop on the fringe of urban areas or near roads or public footpaths are obviously reckless. There is a risk of the bullet missing or going through its intended target and killing someone in its path, and consequently the stalker may be faced with a charge of manslaughter. Charges of manslaughter have also been brought when firearms which were thought to be unloaded have been pointed at people and gone off accidentally. So, serious criminal offences will be considered in cases where the reckless and negligent handling of a gun results in death or serious injury. In addition civil liability would apply, with a possible claim for loss of life or injury through negligence.

In some cases liability may be incurred by a corporate body, an employer or the owner of land, which could include a syndicate or deer management group, e.g. when such bodies have failed to take appropriate action to remedy situations where risks have been exposed. Even if they escape the rigours of the criminal law they may remain liable at civil law if their acts or omissions are negligent and in breach of a duty of care to the victim. The law is more likely to infer a breach where there is an employer/employee relationship, not least because of the normal obligations imposed on employers, including the provision of safe systems of work, proper equipment and training.

Whether a deer management group is a corporate body for this purpose will depend on its constitution. For example a group of adjoining landowners with a common interest in the deer cull who are not formally constituted as a club would be unlikely to have a corporate responsibility. However a group with a formal constitution which provides direction, training and guidance to stalkers and landowners may incur some liability, particularly if formal contracts exist.

Clearly there is a need for stalkers and management groups to seek advice in respect of their potential liabilities. Membership of organisations such as the B.A.S.C. and the Countryside Alliance will provide access to such advice. It is also vital that management groups and individuals carry public liability insurance. Membership of organisations often provides insurance cover for individuals, who should ensure that the policy meets their needs.

Owners and occupiers of land

Owners and occupiers of land where stalking takes place should be aware of their liabilities in respect of visiting stalkers. They have a legal duty not to cause injury by negligence to anyone entering the land, including stalkers. In some circumstances it may also include uninvited guests. There may also be health and safety issues to be considered.[109] In certain circumstances the stalker may be treated as an occupier and therefore have certain responsibilities within the law.

The Occupiers' Liability Act, 1957 (England and Wales) imposes on the occupier of premises[110] a common duty of care to all visitors: that is to take such care as is reasonable in the circumstances to ensure

109. See page 148.
110. 'Premises' means any property of the owner.

the visitor's safety in using the premises for the purpose for which he is invited or permitted by the occupier to be there. In practical terms, this does not mean the occupier has to go to elaborate lengths, but if there are dangers on the property where stalkers have legal access, then he must take reasonable steps to safeguard them from the danger. This is particularly important where a danger is not obvious, e.g. a mine shaft or well hidden in the undergrowth.[111]

The Occupiers' Liability Act, 1984 (England and Wales) imposes on occupiers a duty of care to persons other than visitors and in some circumstances this may extend to those who may not have lawful authority to be on the land or premises where they may be exposed to danger. Owners may not place trespassers in deliberate danger from which they may be injured. For example, actions to deter deer poachers must be reasonable and the setting of any trap or device from which they are likely to be injured as a result will incur civil if not criminal liability. The test would be whether a humane person with the knowledge, ability and resources of the occupier could and would take steps to protect trespassers from any danger on the land.

The Occupiers' Liability (Scotland) Act, 1960, embraces similar principles to those in the Acts covering England and Wales and states that the care should in all circumstances of the case be reasonable to see that a person will not suffer injury or damage by reason of any such danger. The occupier owes the same duty of care to all classes of persons entering his premises, unlike in England and Wales where a distinction is drawn between visitors and trespassers.

In the case of McCluskey v. Lord Advocate damages were sought from the Forestry Commission for injuries caused resulting from a fall on a rocky path used as a short cut between two paths. The action was dismissed and the Commission absolved on the basis of the evidence the rocky path was clearly not part of the official path system, and its condition was obvious. It had been used for many years without accident and did not in terms of the Act constitute a danger. The Commission was under no duty to take steps to prevent members of the public from straying off the official path and the claimant had to be taken as having willingly accepted any risks in doing so.

High seats are an obvious source of danger and should be well maintained. They should be carefully sited to give an unobstructed field of shooting and a solid back stop. The rungs of wooden ladders should be properly secured and not just supported by nails or screws.

111. The Mines and Quarries Act, 1954, requires such dangers as quarries to be fenced and mines to be closed off etc.

147

Make sure your rifle is unloaded before climbing up or down the ladder and in winter be especially mindful of the problems of ice forming on the ladder rungs and rails.

Where there is public access to the area the ladder should be detached after use to prevent children from reaching the seat. You may also consider placing signs to warn of the danger.

Where a stalker falls from a seat through his own fault rather than because of a defective seat or ladder then the occupier is not liable. The stalker has willingly accepted the risks involved and the occupier has a right to expect that such a person will appreciate and guard against any such risks involved in stalking.

If the stalker holds the sporting rights he may also be classed as an occupier, in addition to the landowner. Should a third party be injured then joint liability may exist in respect of any high seats erected by the stalker. Alternatively if the stalker is not classed as an occupier, the claim may be against the owner, who may then have a counter-claim against the stalker who erected the seat.

Liability may be incurred in situations where children play on high seats and become injured, even if the seats are safe and well maintained. The Act states that an occupier must be prepared for children to be less careful than adults and consequently in some circumstances occupiers may need to guard against their use by children.

Health and safety at work

Employers must take reasonable care to protect their employees from risks of foreseeable injury, disease or death at work. If they do not, an employee may be in a position to take civil action and sue for negligence under the common law or breach of a statutory duty under health and safety law. This is of particular relevance to deer stalking, where the risks involving the use of firearms and associated equipment can be high. The risk in some areas of contracting Lyme disease through tick bites should also be considered; employers have a responsibility to provide protective clothing. In addition employees also have responsibilities for their own health and safety and for that of other people who may be put at risk by their work or undertaking.

An employer's duties under common law were identified in general terms in the case of Wilson & Clyde Coal Co. Ltd v. English (1938).[112] All employers should provide and maintain, a safe place of work, safe appliances and equipment, a safe system for doing the work and competent and safety-conscious personnel. These principles are now enshrined in statute law.

The legislation which now protects an employee's rights and general health and safety is considerable, and much of it applies to the recreational stalker with responsibilities for deer management, as well as to the professional stalker. We do not intend to deal here with this legislation in detail, but rather to raise the awareness of stalkers and employers of the aspects of their activities in which there may be health and safety considerations and provide reference to further reading.

The legislation would not generally apply to recreational stalkers who are not *employed* and have no responsibilities for deer management. However, stalkers who conduct an undertaking involving the use of firearms have a legal duty under the Health and Safety at Work etc. Act, 1974, to take all reasonably practical measures so that no one is put at risk. In this sense an 'undertaking' does not necessarily need to involve employment or commercial gain.

The duty may extend to a wide range of other individuals, including gamekeepers, beaters and guests. It is apparent that where the stalker has responsibility for the management of deer involving the use of firearms this will be classed as an undertaking within the legislation. Employers will also have responsibilities where equipment is loaned to a stalker – e.g. chain saws and brush cutters borrowed for clearing rides.

The Health and Safety Executive (H.E.S.) provides extensive guidance in many areas of the law and the use of equipment likely to be used by stalkers. Therefore, in the first instance, information and guidance should be sought from one of their regional branch offices, the B.A.S.C. or the B.D.S.

---

112. AC57 2AER 628.

The Health and Safety at Work etc. Act, 1974

This Act covers employers, all people at work including the self-employed, and the suppliers of equipment to be used at work. It is aimed at people and their activities rather than premises and processes. As we have said, the legislation covers those who 'conduct an undertaking' and will therefore affect many deer stalkers.

The legislation includes provision for both the protection of people at work and the prevention of risks to the health and safety of the general public that may arise from work activities. The main provisions are as follows.

Section 2 states that it is the duty of every employer, so far as is reasonably practicable, to ensure the health, safety and welfare of employees. Provisions and steps that the employer is obliged to take to ensure this condition are detailed in the Act, and include such matters as: the provision and maintenance of equipment; the use, handling, storage and transport of articles; and the provision of information and training.

Section 2(3) provides that employers with five or more workers must have a written statement of their health and safety policy and this must be revised as appropriate. It must set out the general policy with respect to the health and safety at work of employees and the organisation.

Under sections 3 and 4, employers must ensure, as far as is reasonably practicable, that their business does not put at risk people who are not in their employment. Employers must ensure that premises under their control are safe and without risk to persons not in their direct employment.

Under section 6, any person who designs, manufactures, imports or supplies any article for use at work has a responsibility to ensure, as far as is reasonably practicable, that it is safe and without risk to health when properly used. Articles must be properly tested and supplied with appropriate information about their use.

The following provision may be of interest to those erecting high seats. Any person who erects or installs any article for use at work must ensure, so far as is reasonably practicable, that nothing about the way it is erected or installed makes it unsafe or a risk to health when properly used. Additional responsibility to prevent falls from high seats is included in the Workplace (Health, Safety and Welfare) Regulations, 1992. Regulation 13 states that, so far as is reasonably practicable, suitable and effective measures shall be taken to prevent anyone falling a distance likely to cause personal injury.

Section 7 imposes a duty on all employees while at work to take reasonable care for their health and safety and that of others who may be affected by their acts or omissions, and section 8 provides that no one shall intentionally or recklessly interfere with or misuse anything provided for health and safety purposes.

The Noise at Work Regulations, 1989

These regulations, introduced in 1990, are accompanied by a number of guides by the H.S.E. They provide for the protection of workers against risks related to exposure to noise, which no doubt would include the blast from the stalker's rifle.

Under regulation 6 a general duty is placed on every employer to reduce the risk of damage to the hearing of their employees due to exposure to noise to the lowest level reasonably practicable. Regulation 8 deals with the provision of suitable and sufficient ear protection, which employers are obliged to supply where daily noise levels are likely to be a health risk. Varying noise levels, measured in decibels, determine the level of responsibilities placed on employers.

The Personal Protective Equipment at Work Regulations, 1992

These regulations cover all aspects of the provision, maintenance and use of personal protective equipment (P.P.E.) at work and in other circumstances. Under the regulation P.P.E. has a broad meaning and covers all equipment which is intended to be worn or held by a person at work to protect from the risks to health and safety. It includes clothing affording protection against the weather which may be of interest to professional stalkers.

Under regulation 4, every employer shall ensure that suitable P.P.E. is provided to their employees who may be exposed to a risk to their health and safety. It will not be considered suitable unless it is appropriate to the risks involved, takes account of ergonomic requirements and the state of health of the person and, so far as practicable, is effective when worn. This would apply to protective clothing required in deer larders.

OTHER STALKING LIABILITIES

There are also stalking liabilities involved in the following, which are elaborated upon in the relevant chapters as indicated:
- claims for compensation in respect of crop damage – chapter 4
- trespass – chapter 8
- firearm security and safekeeping – chapter 6
- disposing of animal by-products – chapter 5
- dealing with poachers – chapter 9
- sending trophies by post – chapter 5.

CHAPTER 8

Trespass and Deer

If you have responsibilities for deer management, have wild deer on your land or keep farmed deer, then the issues surrounding the civil wrongdoing known as trespass, will no doubt arise. Retrieving shot deer over boundaries, poachers, farmed deer escaping and deer hounds unlawfully encroaching onto land are just a few examples of situations involving trespass. Public consultation over the right to roam in the countryside may also lead in the future to increased public access in areas where deer management is necessary and therefore it is useful to have a clear understanding of the issues involved.

Legislation on access in Scotland is likely in the near future. After discussions in the Access Forum in December 1998, Scottish Natural Heritage advised the government on the shape of future legislation; the main features of the advice were that a new right of access to land should be created, to be exercised with responsibility, and that work should be done on drawing up a new Scottish Countryside Code to give definition to the duties and responsibilities of all concerned. Scotland has its own legislature and the anticipated introduction of access legislation will have implications for stalkers.

Simple trespass, which is known as a tort (a delict in Scotland) is an unlawful act under civil law. It is not a crime except in certain circumstances provided for by statute law, such as trespass on railway property. Generally, recourse for simple trespass is through the

152

county courts, where compensation in appropriate cases may be awarded to the aggrieved party.

Trespass may take many forms. It is not confined to merely trespassing on land, but may also involve persons and property. Despite the myths that abound, many of the principles of trespass apply just as much to Scotland as they do to England and Wales, although some differences exist. Public debate about increased public access to the countryside in both Scotland and England has invited comparisons between the law in the two jurisdictions.

TRESPASS BY PEOPLE

Trespass is not restricted to a person's physical entry or presence on land where he has no right to be, but also to placing or throwing any material object upon the land. Land in this context includes not only the surface, but everything fixed to it such as buildings, everything beneath it and the air space above it. It also includes water. An act of civil trespass would even extend to the situation where someone makes a constructive, rather than physical, entry into land – e.g. a stalker firing a rifle from land where lawful authority is granted into land where permission has not been sought.[113] Trespass is still committed even if someone does not physically touch the land – e.g. driving a vehicle onto the land. In this latter example a criminal offence of driving a vehicle elsewhere than on a road may be committed, contrary the Road Traffic Act.

The term 'lawful authority' may embrace a number of different situations where someone may claim a right to be on the land if challenged. When in dispute it is usually the landowner or occupier who is approached to confirm whether permission has been granted and not withdrawn. Permission may also be conditional or relate to a number of persons – e.g. members of a deer management group viewing deer on a certain date. When gaining access to land for sporting purposes such as stalking, permission should ideally be in writing. Indeed the grant of a firearm certificate may depend on this.[114]

There will often be a sporting lease, and this should be carefully examined when it is taken up, to ensure that there are no misunderstandings which are likely to give rise to inadvertent trespass. It is advisable to make use of definitive maps with clearly marked

113. See chapter 7 on stalking the boundary.
114. See chapter 6.

boundaries of your area.[115] Stalkers who hold legal sporting rights over land which is let to a tenant have lawful authority to be on the land for those sporting purposes even if this is against the tenant's wishes.

'Lawful authority' also includes using private and public rights of way. These provide a right of access to the land without the express permission of the landowner. Private rights of way are granted to allow the owner of one property to cross another's land for reasons of access. There are several types of public rights of way. The most common are footpaths, bridleways and roads. All are referred to as 'highways' over which the public have a right to pass and repass. The responsibility for maintenance and signing rests with the highways authority, which may take legal action against anyone who causes obstruction or nuisance on the highway. Care should therefore be taken when erecting deer fencing or high seats to ensure that they are not placed on or near a footpath where obstruction or nuisance is likely to be caused.

Anyone using a right of way may have with them any article regarded as a 'usual accompaniment', such as a walking stick, binoculars or a dog.[116] Dogs should be under close control – at heel or ideally on a lead. Whatever the item carried or pushed it should not cause a nuisance or damage. Where rifles are being carried on a right of way to gain access to land where permission has been granted to stalk, it is advisable that they are carried within their slips and are unloaded (a rifle may still be deemed as loaded if bullets are left in the magazine).[117]

Poachers who claim they were on a highway or footpath when they indulged in their activities will find such a defence rejected by the courts. A number of past cases have held that using a right of way for an unlawful purpose may still be treated as trespassing. A footpath or right of way must be used for the purpose for which it is intended, i.e. to pass and repass as a means of communication.[118] Therefore a stalker who shoots a deer from a footpath on land where permission has not been granted would be trespassing with a firearm in addition to his poaching activities.[119] The latter situation is an example of where the tort of trespass to land forms an essential part of a criminal offence. However there are many situations in which trespassers may be acting unlawfully without the need to prove trespass.

115. See chapter 7.
116. R. v. Mathias, 1861. In this case a pram was referred to as such.
117. See chapter 6.
118. R. v. Pratt, 1855, and Harrison v. Duke of Rutland, 1893.
119. See chapters 6 and 9.

The fact that the criminal law makes exceptions for certain activities does not negate an individual's liability against trespass. For example, the picking of wild mushrooms is allowed in certain circumstances by the Theft Act, 1968, so you may not be stealing, but if you do so without the landowner's permission you are trespassing. A person who wanders aimlessly about the land, without lawful authority, searching for cast antlers for example, also commits a trespass, irrespective of the rights of ownership of the antlers found.[120]

Common Law in England and Wales

A person who enters or remains on land without lawful authority commits trespass against the holder of the land and this would include any interference with the land. This type of trespass would be actionable in itself, even if damage is not caused, as the landowner would be able to take civil action via the County Court.

Common Law in Scotland

The view has sometimes been expressed that in contrast to the position in England there is no law of trespass in Scotland. That view is wrong, but it may, perhaps, result from misunderstandings about the following points:

- In Scotland, trespass is a civil wrong at Common Law. The Scottish Common Law of civil wrongs is called the Law of Delict, and corresponds to the Law of Tort in England. Delict, in contrast to Tort, did not develop from the notion of trespass in the much wider sense in which it was historically used in English law; 'trespass to a chattel', for example, would not have any meaning in Scots law. However, the word 'trespass' was introduced from England to Scotland, and has been in common usage for perhaps two centuries.
- It is a general principle of the Law of Delict that so far as property is concerned, it is necessary to prove loss or damage in order to ground an action for damages. Thus, if trespass results in no loss or damage, no action for damages will lie. It must be stressed that this reflects a general principle of the law; it is not a condition special to the law concerning trespass.

An interdict in Scotland corresponds to an injunction in England. A lawful occupier may ask either the Sheriff or the Court of Session to

120. See chapter 1.

grant an interdict against a trespasser. But it must be kept in mind that it is a discretionary remedy, granted only when the action the pursuer (corresponding to the plaintiff in England) seeks to prohibit is of some consequence, or there is a danger of repetition which there is good reason to seek to prevent (for example, because there is reason to conclude that it could give rise to a disturbance).

Dealing with trespassers

People who persistently trespass can pose problems in terms of both deer management and safety. Deer change their habits when faced with too much human pressure. Some, especially fallow, can become almost nocturnal. They then become difficult to manage and so unwanted trespassers become a nuisance, particularly in areas where culling is necessary. Areas of natural beauty often hold large numbers of deer and people seeking recreation, particularly in the Highlands, often impede professional stalkers in achieving their culls. This can be a serious problem during the hind season on the lower ground when in January and February there is the opportunity to cull beasts emerging from cover.

Apart from the obvious disruption to stalking activities caused by someone being in the wrong place at the wrong time, the most serious potential risk is to human life itself, from a stray bullet. Whilst safe and responsible shooting should be a stalker's absolute priority, accidents can and do happen.[121]

Whilst the chances of such an accident may seem remote, keeping a watchful eye out for trespassers and dealing with them effectively will lessen the risks of accident or disruption. Some trespassers may simply be lost or unaware that they are trespassing on private property, others may pose an additional threat of poaching. Although poaching is generally done during the hours of darkness, reconnaissance is often done on foot during the preceding days.[122] You may recognise your local poacher, in which case your approach will be better informed, but on many occasions you will be dealing with someone you do not know and therefore your actions must be carefully considered, with the ultimate aim of an informal resolution.

Owners and occupiers of the land, and anyone acting with their authority, have certain powers to deal with trespassers personally. In the early 1900s one lawyer's advice was as follows:

---

121. Your liability in such a situation is discussed in chapter 7.
122. See chapter 9 for poaching methods.

If you find a man walking down your glades doing no damage to the trees or fences, your only course is to show him the quickest path to the King's highway, and see that he takes it. Should he object to go, use as much force as is necessary, and if he shows fight, and you are strong enough to do so, knock him down, tie his hands and legs, and have him carried off.

Our advice today is rather different, inasmuch as that you should generally resist the temptation to take physical action to remove trespassers. To do so could lead to an argument and may end in violence, and it might invite a counter-claim by the trespasser, who may sue or prosecute for assault. You may request him to leave the land and should allow reasonable time for him to do so by the most convenient route to the right of way. The Common Law does allow you physically to remove trespassers who refuse to leave but, should you do so it is essential that you use no more force than is reasonable and necessary in the circumstances. You have no power to require them to supply their names and addresses, which presents obvious practical difficulties in pursuing any legal action.

Where legal action is taken in England and Wales, the landowner may apply to the court for both damages and an injunction. The effect of such an injunction is that the trespasser becomes liable for contempt of court should he trespass again. The court will need to be satisfied that there is a risk of further trespass before granting such an injunction. In Scotland, as referred to earlier, unless actual damage has been suffered, damages are not recoverable for simple trespass, particularly if innocent or unwitting. Interdicts are granted at the discretion of the court, which would have to be satisfied that there was reasonable apprehension that the trespass would be repeated in the future.

In cases which do not involve a crime the police, if called, are powerless. They can neither remove the trespassers nor demand their names and addresses, and if they do intervene they may not be acting in the execution of their duty. However, they may remain to ensure that there are no breaches of the peace. Landowners or persons acting on their authority must ensure that their own conduct is not threatening or violent towards trespassers, nor should they intimidate genuine ramblers on a right of way. Should they do so the police may be obliged to get involved, particularly where actual or threatened violence is used.

Criminal trespass

The Trespass (Scotland) Act, 1865, and the Public Order Act, 1986, create criminal offences of trespass by occupation of private property when taking up some form of residence such as camping. The offences are committed where the consent of the owner or occupier has not been given and they vary in respect of specific conditions that have to be met. The legislation provides the police with powers of arrest without warrant against those committing offences. A toleration policy is exercised in relation to traditional travelling people in areas where the provision of sites is inadequate, but this does not extend to large groups of people whose size, pattern and purpose of encampment are unrelated to established traveller movement, such as 'peace convoys'.

Aggravated trespass

The early nineties saw increasing concern over the activities of a number of groups and individuals intent on disrupting country sports. There were fears for the impact on rural economies of long-term disruption; for many people employed in rural areas their livelihood was at stake. Those concerns were not restricted to anti-blood sport campaigners; angling matches and even the Grand National had suffered disruption. There were frequent complaints that the police were uncertain of their powers or unwilling to use them, and that the law was inadequate. Hence legislation was seen as necessary to protect people who were conducting lawful activity in the countryside. What emerged was the Criminal Justice and Public Order Act, 1994, which not only created an offence of aggravated trespass but also addressed a number of other issues concerning trespass, including the problems caused by New Age travellers and ravers.

Under section 68 of this Act, a person commits the offence of aggravated trespass if, whilst trespassing on land, they do anything with intent to disrupt or obstruct a lawful activity, or seek to intimidate someone so as to deter him from engaging in a lawful activity. An 'activity' is lawful for the purposes of this section if those engaged in it do so without committing any offences and are themselves not trespassing.

Accidental or inadvertent trespass (including that by hunts) would not be an offence, even if it actually does cause disruption of a lawful activity, provided that the trespasser does not *intend* the disruption.

The trespass must be on land in the open air, and metalled roads are not included. However, it would apply if a footpath or other right of way was used for the purpose of disruption. It is quite possible that the offence of aggravated trespass may be committed by someone disrupting or attempting to disrupt deer management activity, particularly stalking, provided of course everything was lawful, i.e. the stalkers themselves were not trespassing, firearm certificates were correct and the deer being shot were in season.

Section 69 gives the police powers to remove persons committing or participating in aggravated trespass. An offence is committed where a person fails to leave the land as soon as practicable or having left returns within a period of three months. The police have a power of arrest in these circumstances.

TRESPASS BY DEER

Deer that are truly wild, *ferae naturae* are ownerless[123] and therefore cannot trespass, since in the wild state they are free to roam where they please. However, concerns arise over damage to the natural environment and crops caused by unnaturally high wild deer stocks.

Historically an unchecked increase in deer numbers did not incur any liability on behalf of the occupier, even if resultant damage was caused to a neighbour's crops. However, in recent years the density of our wild deer populations has become acute in some areas of Scotland. Legislation has increased the powers of the Deer Commission for Scotland, enabling them to dictate cull levels and if necessary take action to reduce deer numbers. In these circumstances persons acting under such authority would not commit acts of trespass even if they were acting against the owner's wishes.[124] The owner of the land may also be liable for any expenses incurred by the Deer Commission in carrying out such action subject to certain conditions. The situation south of the border is also of concern, with a number of different bodies working towards maintaining a sustainable level of deer numbers in the interests of our natural environment.

Deer in captivity, whether from wild stock or captive-bred, can commit trespass and therefore their owners are liable in certain circumstances. Where untagged captive deer have strayed onto the open hill rights of ownership may become difficult to prove.[125] It has long been established that landowners have a duty to ensure that any livestock, including captive deer are adequately fenced in.

---

123. See chapter 1.
124. See chapter 3.
125. See chapter 1.

The Animals Act, 1971 (England and Wales), and the Animals Act, (Scotland), 1987, make provision for strict liability for damage caused by animals including situations where livestock and other animals have strayed onto another's land. Deer are included in both Acts. Hitherto such liabilities were dealt with, in part, by old legislation and the Common Law. The latter still applies in respect of an ordinary duty of care upon owners to ensure their animals do not cause injury, damage or nuisance, including the death of, or injury to, any person. Such liabilities are dealt with in detail in chapter 1.

The Animals Act, 1971 (England and Wales)

This Act identifies liability in respect of the owners of trespassing livestock, which includes 'deer not in the wild state'. Under section 4, where deer belonging to any person stray onto another person's land and: a) damage is done by the deer to the land or any property on it which is in the ownership or occupation of the other person, or: b) any expenses are reasonably incurred by that other person in keeping the deer while they cannot be restored to the owner or while they are detained in pursuance of section 7 (see below) or in ascertaining to whom they belong. The person to whom the deer belong is liable for the damage and expense incurred. For the purposes of this section any deer 'belong' to the person in whose possession they are, but would not include the person detaining the trespassing deer.

An exemption from liability under this section would apply if it could be shown that the damage was due wholly to the fault of the person suffering it, but it would not include a failure by that person to fence their land adequately.

Under section 7, where it is clear that the deer are not from the wild state and have strayed onto land where they could be said to be trespassing and are not under the control of any person then the occupier of the land is entitled to detain the deer subject to the following conditions, unless ordered to return them by a court:

- where deer are detained in pursuance of this section the right to detain them would cease at the end of a period of forty-eight hours, unless within that period notice of the detention has been given to the police and also to the owner of the deer, if known
- the right to detain them would cease when a sufficient amount of money is given to the person detaining the deer to satisfy any claim he may have
- if he has no such claim, the right would cease when the deer are claimed by the owner

Where deer have been detained in pursuance of this section for a period of not less than fourteen days the person detaining them may sell them at a market or at public auction, unless proceedings are pending for the return of the deer or for any claim under section 4 (see above). Where deer are sold in these circumstances the proceeds of the sale, less the costs of the damage and expenses incurred, are recoverable by the original owner.

A person detaining trespassing deer is liable for any damage caused to them through a failure to treat them with reasonable care or supply them with adequate food and water while so detained.

Section 8 imposes a duty on those who own deer to take such care as is reasonable to ensure that damage is not caused by the animals straying onto a highway. Where damage is caused by animals straying from unfenced land they will not be regarded as having breached this duty of care if the land is common land or situated in an area where fencing is not customary or where a right exists to place them on that land.

The Animals (Scotland) Act, 1987

Section 1 of this Act provides that keepers of certain animals are liable for any damage caused by their foraging. Deer are included as being likely, unless controlled or restrained, to damage to a material extent land or the produce of land, whether harvested or not. However, under section 2, a person shall not be liable if the damage done was due wholly to the fault of the person sustaining it or if they had willingly accepted the risk as theirs.

Section 3 states that where animals stray onto any land, other than the highway, and are not under the control of any person, the occupier of the land may detain them for the purpose of preventing injury or damage. Part VI of the Civic Government (Scotland) Act, 1982, relating to lost and abandoned property applies in relation to any animals, other than stray dogs, which are detained in these circumstances, in the same way as to any property taken under section 67 of that Act and subject to some amendment of section 74.

Effectively this means that where such animals have been detained and it is reasonable to infer that they have been lost or abandoned the finder should take reasonable care of them and without unreasonable delay report the fact to the owner or the police, who are obliged to take reasonable steps to ascertain the owner if he is not known. The Chief Constable may make such arrangements as he considers appropriate for the care and custody of the animals. Practically this may well involve the finder being requested to care and have custody of the animals. In this situation, under section 74, provided the animals have been detained for a period of two months and not claimed, the person shall become the owner of the animals. The rights of the original owners following disposal of animals, compensation and appeals are also detailed in the above Act.

DOGS AND TRESPASS

There are many situations involving trespass where the welfare of deer is jeopardised, particularly where dogs are involved. The owners of trespassing dogs can be liable for their animals' misdemeanours and there have been a number of successful civil actions in such cases.

In Scotland the use of dogs to take or pursue deer is prohibited.[126] This is not the case in England and Wales, where deer hounds or coursing dogs can be used against deer.[127] In these circumstances, where trespass on land occurs a legal exemption from the criminal offence of trespass in search or pursuit of game including hares and rabbits applies,[128] provided it can be shown that the trespass occurred whilst in fresh pursuit of a deer, hare or fox found elsewhere, on land on which permission to hunt or course had been granted. However, as far as the civil law is concerned, no such protection exists and those in charge of the dogs are liable for their trespasses and also any followers who may have unintentionally found themselves on land where permission had not been obtained.

Civil action against the masters of deer hounds is not uncommon, particularly in the West Country, where a number of private landowners, including the National Trust, have now refused hunts permission to go on their land. Their wishes should be respected by all those who pursue such activities. If they are not, action can be taken, under the criminal law for poaching and under the civil law for trespass. Where a hunt knowingly enters land without the consent of the owner or occupier in search or pursuit of deer, an offence

126. See chapter 3.
127. See chapter 2.
128. Game Act, 1831, section 35.

under section 1(1) or (2) of the Deer Act, 1991, is committed, with no protection from section 35 of the Game Act, 1831.

In 1985 the League Against Cruel Sports took civil action for trespass against the Devon and Somerset Staghounds following a number of invasions of one of their deer sanctuaries. An injunction was granted at Bristol High Court and damages were awarded to the League. The judge defined trespass by hunts as follows:

> The Master will be liable for trespass if he intended to cause hounds to enter such land, or if by failure to exercise proper control over them he caused them to enter such land.[129]

This case has been followed by a number of similar actions over more recent years. The legal definition of liability here could be applied to any individual who allows dogs to enter land where permission has not been granted, although it is doubtful whether civil action against someone merely exercising his dog would be worthwhile – there are other options that should be explored in this situation, as described earlier in respect of persons trespassing on land.

Shooting trespassing dogs

Taking summary action by shooting a trespassing dog rather than using the legal system may well put you at risk of court action. Dogs are classed as property and shooting a dog, even in the act of chasing a deer, may render you liable to prosecution for criminal damage or a civil claim – and the latter could be hefty if the dog is found to be a Crufts champion!

The Criminal Damage Act, 1971, covers offences of damage committed in England and Wales. In Scotland there is a Common Law offence of damage and an offence of vandalism under section 78 of the Criminal Justice (Scotland) Act, 1980; these are virtually identical to the offences contained in the English law.

Section 1 of the Criminal Damage Act, 1971, states:

> A person who without lawful excuse destroys or damages any property belonging to another intending to destroy or damage such property or being reckless as to whether any such property would be destroyed or damaged shall be guilty of an offence.

---

129. League Against Cruel Sports v. Scott and others.

Shooting a dog chasing or attacking wild deer on your land would be difficult to defend as you would have to show lawful excuse for your actions – i.e. that you shot the dog to protect your property or a right or interest in it. (The defence is dealt with in detail later in respect of captive deer.) We know of one case that was successfully defended at Petworth Magistrates' Court in 1974, but this is not considered to be a sound authority.

Generally wild deer are not classed as 'property' and therefore a defence would have to rely on convincing the court that the sporting rights to the deer were a right or interest in property, which includes 'any right or privilege in or over the land, whether created by grant, licence or otherwise'. It could be argued that killing a dog in these circumstances is an attempt to protect the wild deer which the holder of the sporting rights has a right to take and that a dog chasing or killing deer in these circumstances does not threaten that right since the sporting rights remain intact. A court may consider whether the action taken was reasonable in the circumstances.

Dogs worrying farm or park deer

There is no express legal right to shoot a dog in any circumstances, even if it is caught worrying livestock. However, under the Animals Act, 1971, which does not apply in Scotland, you are entitled to take action to protect livestock. Fortunately, deer that are not in the wild state are included in the definition of 'livestock', so effectively the following defence against any civil proceedings would apply in all cases where a dog was shot chasing deer that were captive in a park or farm. Similar provisions apply in Scotland under the Animals (Scotland) Act, 1987, which includes not only livestock but any animal whilst in captivity.

Under section 9(1) and section 4 (Scotland) there is a defence in any civil proceedings for those who shoot dogs worrying livestock, if the court is satisfied that:

- the person acted for the protection of any livestock
- he was entitled to do so
- the police were notified within forty-eight hours

Under section 9(2) a person is entitled to protect livestock if the livestock or the land belongs to him, or he is acting with the owner's authority. The entitlement does not extend to the killing of a dog worrying livestock which has strayed onto land and the dog belongs to the occupier of that land or is on the land with the occupier's permission.

164

Under section 9(3)(4), a person may only act for the protection of any livestock if he has reasonable grounds to believe that:

- the dog is worrying or is about to worry and there are no other reasonable means of ending or preventing the worrying
- the dog has been worrying livestock, has not left the vicinity and is not under the control of any person and there are no practical means of ascertaining to whom it belongs

The above only provides for protection against civil proceedings. Should a charge of criminal damage be made for shooting a dog then the defendant would need to prove he had a lawful excuse. This may be possible, since the deer in these circumstances would be classed as property and the criminal law provides for the protection of property in circumstances where it is at risk of being damaged or destroyed. In this situation the deer may be injured or killed by a chasing or attacking dog and you would have a lawful excuse under the Criminal Damage Act, 1971, to take action provided the following conditions were met:

- it was believed the consent of the owner of the dog had been given or would have been given in such circumstances
- your actions were taken in order to protect the deer or a right or interest in it and at the time you believed the deer were in immediate need of protection and the means of protection adopted were reasonable having regard to all the circumstances

This means you would have to justify your actions and if it could be shown that other means were at your disposal to stop the dog, rather than by shooting, then your defence might be weakened.

TRESPASS AND PROPERTY

A form of trespass can be committed against property, where perhaps the criteria for a criminal offence of either damage or theft are not satisfied. It is known as 'trespass to goods'. This is the intentional or negligent interference with the possession of another's property. The interference must be direct and forcible, although a mere touching, unless accidental, may constitute a trespass in some circumstances. Such trespasses are actionable *per se*, in that a case could be pursued at civil court.

There are many situations where those who manage deer or possess sporting rights may be affected by such trespass. The meaning of goods is very wide and would include any article in the possession or constructive possession of another.[130] This would include captive or farmed deer that are interfered with in some way or released. High seats and signs relating to deer management are often moved or interfered with, and all such acts constitute a trespass to goods. It is not essential for the person to know his actions were wrong, provided they are intentional or negligent.

It is perhaps worth summarising a few general points about trespass.

- in practice, actions for damages for trespass are rare. If it happens that the lawful occupier of land can identify a trespasser as being responsible for loss or damage to his property, he may make a complaint of vandalism to the police where circumstances justify that course
- a lawful occupier of land may require any person who is on his land without legal right or permission to leave at any time. It is fair to say, however, that very few occupiers or land managers will require someone to leave their land without good reason
- questions are sometimes asked about the use of force to remove a trespasser. While there is some legal authority for saying that force may be used, general advice must be that in the absence of absolute necessity it should not. There are obvious risks involved; even with the best intentions, a situation may develop in a quite unexpected way, and get out of hand. If a trespasser will not respond positively to a polite request to leave, and there is a definite immediate need for him to go, the police should be asked for advice or assistance

---

130. In a case at Peterborough in 1993, the County Court ruled that the blowing of a hunting horn to disrupt hounds amounted to a trespass to goods.

CHAPTER 9

Poaching

Poaching is one of the oldest professions, and centuries of experience have developed numerous methods of killing deer, including bows, snares, traps, dogs, firearms and even spikes on trees. The race to take deer before being discovered by the landowner or gamekeeper still results in immense cruelty. Indiscriminate poachers have no concern for the wellbeing of the deer or for risks to public health from ill-prepared venison. They have but one aim – a quick and easy profit.

POACHING PAST AND PRESENT

Until the tenth century, hunting in Britain was deemed as a necessity of life rather than a sport. The Saxons were keen to follow hounds on foot, mainly for the purpose of pest control. It was at this time that the kings started to designate areas of common folkland as hunting grounds and to strengthen game laws. The full nature of these laws is not known but Canute decreed that every man had the right to hunt on his land, establishing a principle which remains today.

The Normans enforced the Saxon laws after the invasion, but placed the forests under the sole jurisdiction of the King, preserving game for sport and feeding the royal household. William the Conqueror brought law and order to the land, 'so that a man could travel unmolested with his bosom full of gold and no man dare slay another'. Penalties could be extreme: a man who lay with a woman against her will was destined 'to forfeit those members with which he had disported himself'. Castration was not reserved for the rapist alone. William regarded hunting as a royal prerogative and imposed the strict continental forest laws to protect that right. Although the full nature of these laws is unknown he certainly introduced castration, amputation and blinding for 'venison trespass'.

The poacher's dog was not immune from such barbaric treatment either. As a preventative measure large dogs were 'lawed', a source of considerable grievance for people living in and near the forests. It is presumed the dogs were not too pleased either for those too tall to pass through the lawing ring, 18 inches and a barley corn high, had three toes of the front foot removed with a two inch chisel. Effectively lame, the dog could not chase and bring down the King's deer. There is a tale of one resourceful individual who trained a pig to retrieve game as a means of evading the forest laws against dogs.

Poaching with bow and arrow

The most common weapon over the years has undoubtedly been the bow. There have been many examples of its use, and not just against deer. In recent years a gamekeeper in North Yorkshire was shot in the chest with a bolt from a poacher's crossbow. Luckily he survived to tell the tale; others have not been so fortunate.

An early account of poaching with a longbow in England dates back to 1228, and took place in Rockingham Forest. The foresters, acting on information received, set an ambush and caught four out of five greyhounds that were hunting. On their return to the forest they saw four men with longbows and one with a crossbow, standing behind trees waiting for deer to be driven past them. They were challenged but made a fighting retreat. One of the foresters was killed by an arrow to the left breast 'to the depth of a hand slantwise'. The poachers escaped in the dark, and the villagers apparently all swore they did not recognise the dogs.

Thomas de Bromlegh, described as 'a very frequent malefactor of venison' was found armed in Kinver Forest. When challenged by the foresters he climbed into an oak tree and shot arrows at them. But this was a tactical error as they had him surrounded and outnumbered. Eventually he was taken by force and imprisoned in Bridgenorth Castle.

Both the longbow and the crossbow appear to have been in use for many years as weapons to take deer illegally. These have obvious advantages for poachers: they are almost silent when compared to the rifle, and the penalty for being caught in possession is minimal, as they are not classed as firearms. However the use of bow and arrow to take any animal or bird is outlawed in the U.K. under the Wildlife and Countryside Act, 1981, and the Wildlife (Northern Ireland) Order, 1985.

Bows are not as restricted in other countries. In the United States hunting deer with the conventional longbow and arrow has become increasingly popular, although it is strictly controlled and subject to appropriate licences in most states. A good deal of legal specification exists in relation to both the power of the bows and type of arrows used. Hunting with crossbows appears to be rather more restricted and in some states is completely banned.

It is the crossbow that in recent times has become the popular poacher's weapon. It is not difficult to imagine why as they can be accurate and extremely powerful. They are versatile and can be easily transported and carried without detection. During the 1980s there were many incidents involving their misuse; in one year there were eleven reported cases, which included two suicides and many pitiful injuries to animals.

Public pressure to legislate against the use of crossbows resulted in the Crossbows Act, 1987. It does not apply to crossbows with a drawn weight of less than 1.4 kilograms. It is an offence to sell or hire a crossbow to someone under the age of seventeen. If such a person buys or hires a crossbow or part of one, he also commits an offence. He may possess a crossbow, however, if supervised by someone who is twenty-one or over.

The Act gives various powers to the police to enable them to prove unlawful possession, including the searching of a suspect or vehicle and the power to enter land to conduct such a search. The courts are also given powers of forfeiture and disposal of crossbows in such cases brought before them.

The chances of any bow being used in a humane manner by unscrupulous poachers are remote. The vast majority just could not care less. If their ratio of success is one in five they are happy. Crossbows are still being used in some parts of the country and care should be exercised in approaching anyone suspected of their possession.

Gang poaching and the Waltham Blacks

The term poaching comes from the French verb *pocher*, to 'encroach' – to be on land where you have no right to be, in search of wild animals. Whilst the term is used to describe the purpose of some Acts relating to game, such as the Night Poaching Act, a definition does not exist in law.

Gang poaching has always been a threat to stocks of fish, game and deer. Two, three or more people may just have been looking to each other for mutual support when afraid of the dark, but at the other extreme might be a band of determined men, faces blackened, white bandages tied to their arms for identification, and armed with guns, sticks and swords. Such a gang was a formidable force in the darkness of a secluded wood, particularly when they had sworn to stand and fight or to shoot any deserting gang member.

One group of deer poachers which was active in 1723 was of such a violent nature that Parliament passed an Act specifically to deal with them. They were known as the Waltham Blacks, a band of thirty or more who met at a secluded inn, deep in Waltham Forest. Supper consisted of 'eighteen dishes of venison in every shape; boiled with broth, roasted, hashed collops, pasties, umble pies and a large haunch in the middle, larded'. Each man had a bottle of claret set at his elbow and the evening was spent merrily with singing and jollity until two in the morning.

Each man was disguised with a blackened face and their leader was known as the Black Prince or Prince Orinoko King of the Blacks. To enter the society one had to be seen drunk on two occasions to establish one's temperament in compliance with the old proverb, 'Women, children and drunken folks speak truth.' The Blacks also attracted criminals who had no settled employment but lived by their 'vices and indulged in all manner of wickedness, robbing, house breaking and in every species of depredation'.

Violence and intimidation became their trademarks. A magistrate committed one of the gang to prison and received a letter demanding the person's release or his house would be fired. The magistrate failed to bend to their will and the gang cut down young oaks to the value of £500. Landowners who refused to hand over money or venison would find cattle maimed, barns and haystacks burned down. One poacher caught in Windsor Park was fined and his gun confiscated. The Blacks assembled at the keeper's cottage and demanded the return of the weapon. The keeper's son looked out of the bedroom window and was shot dead.

The Black Act was a catalogue of the gang's excesses. It created a range of offences based specifically on their activities and included around 350 ways of securing an appointment with the hangman. To have a blackened face whilst thinking of poaching was virtually enough to be proved guilty and executed. The Act was also retrospective in that all persons who had committed such offences were required to surrender themselves and make a full confession giving the names of all accomplices, whereby a free pardon was granted. An order could be issued for their arrest and failing to comply resulted in instant conviction, confiscation of estates and execution.

To ensure a goodly flow of intelligence informers were promised free pardons and all inhabitants of a hundred (a community) were taxed to make good any damage done by offenders against the Act. But for all the power and ferocity of the law the authorities had to resort to subterfuge to trap the leaders. They were tricked into going to London, where they were subsequently arrested. Four were later executed and thirty-six other members were transported overseas.

That was the end of the Waltham Blacks, but not the Black Act. Although it was intended to last for three years, it was thought so useful that it remained in force until 1823 when Sir Robert Peel's Bill repealed nearly all the provisions. Its abrogation heralded a new approach to the problems of crime and punishment but one side-effect was the relegation of poaching offences to the bottom of the league in terms of penalties and enforcement.

The motivation behind poaching

Historically the poacher has been viewed as a romantic folk hero taking from the gentry to feed his family. To be fair, many fended off hunger with fur, fish or fowl and, to a degree, gamekeepers tolerated the 'one for the pot' character. Such minor losses were accepted as long as the poacher's activities were not obvious and did not attract the boss's attention.

Some still see poaching as a victimless rural pursuit, stocking the freezer or making a few pounds at no one's expense. They see wild animals as being ownerless, which they are, but overlook the legal principle that rights to take them are vested in landowners and occupiers. However, commercial poachers kept the London markets stocked with all forms of game, using carriers and the rail networks to speed their unlawful gains out of the county. Their aim was purely profit.

But profit and food are not the only motivation. It is often the thrill of the chase, putting dogs to the ultimate test and evading capture that lures poachers from their beds. We knew a farmer who bred and shot pheasants on his own land, yet on many an early morning his wife would find the kitchen floor littered with pheasants following poaching trips on his cycle. The only gain was the excitement of outwitting the keeper and perhaps getting something for nothing. We have also seen a video taken by a gang of deer poachers lamping for deer with dogs and four-wheel-drive vehicles, where the commentary is highly charged with emotion and the thrill of the chase. Perhaps the law will never overcome such excitement.

Modern trends

If poaching ever had a romantic image it has disappeared from today's country scene. The old village poacher, with a reputation as well known to the local gamekeepers as to his friends, is less evident. There

is a degree of admiration for these old characters, and there is a prolif-
eration of books describing their exploits and methods. But modern
technology has influenced the way deer are poached. The modern
rifle with its telescopic sight, the electric lamp and battery combination and the four-wheel-drive vehicle are the type of equipment now
used to poach deer.

Poaching methods vary across the country, depending on the
terrain, the species of deer and their availability. What may be a
common practice in the Highlands of Scotland may be rare in the
south of England. Poachers vary too; some are semi-professional and
others merely go out because they fancy a bit of venison, some extra
holiday money or simply the thrill of the chase. What is common to
all is their total disrespect for the welfare of deer. Dependent fawns
are often orphaned, killing methods are crude and carcases are never
bled correctly or inspected to detect disease.

Deer poaching in the remote areas of Scotland is more likely to be
done with rifles, either from the vehicle or by the poachers taking to
the hill on foot. They are opportunists who know that in such areas
they are difficult to detect, owing to the vastness and isolation of the
landscape. The rifle is stowed discreetly in the vehicle until deer are
spotted perhaps 200 or 300 metres from the roadside. They are then
shot out of the vehicle window, which provides not only a good lean
for the shooter but a degree of disguise. Unless the area is persistently
poached, the deer will not be too alarmed at the vehicle's presence.
Even if the shot is heard it is unlikely that it can be located quickly
enough to prevent the short drag of the carcase to the vehicle and
escape.

Where poachers take to the hill with rifles a more traditional style
is adopted. The wind, the lie of the ground and roaming sheep all
have to be considered in addition to someone who may be stalking
the poachers themselves. If they are disturbed the rifles will often be
hidden and the poachers will lie up, keep watch and await the
moment to depart or continue. If a deer is shot it is likely to be part
butchered on the spot rather than risk a lengthy and arduous drag
off the hill. The best cuts of venison will be loaded into a bag and
quickly carried back to the vehicle or a rendezvous point. These
poachers are undoubtedly in a different class from those who
operate out of the more industrialised areas of the country. They
will be good shots by necessity, fit and capable of good stalking
techniques.

Apart from these practices in the remote Highlands, the most
common method of deer poaching currently used is coursing by dogs
supported by four-wheel-drive vehicles. At night, with the minimum
use of a high-powered lamp to avoid detection, this cruel method can

be devastatingly effective. Unless you notice vehicle tracks on your land you may never know that deer have been taken until it is too late. This practice is commonly referred to as 'lamping', but unlike the normal practice for vermin control, firearms are rarely used. Access is gained to land via either gateways or insecure fencing. The deer are chased at high speed and lurchers slipped whilst still on the move. The deer are coursed and dragged down, the dogs are quickly called off and the deer are dispatched. Some gangs are even less refined and simply drive their vehicles at the deer, knocking them down and causing untold suffering.

Humane dispatch is rare, with deer being crudely killed by a variety of means. They are then thrown into the vehicle without being gralloched and the poaching continues in areas where deer have not been driven into cover. We know of one gang of poachers who record their exploits on video. It is not uncommon for six or seven deer to be taken per night by this method from one estate, with all gralloching and carcase preparation done elsewhere. They have a ready market for the venison via unscrupulous dealers, the hotel trade and their private outlets. Their own freezers are often full and so are their pockets, with a tax-free income.

These gangs are well organised and will get to know the ground. On the night they may also divert police resources by reporting or creating incidents away from the poaching area.

Not all poaching of deer is quite so blatant and more subtle methods are used – e.g. when a legitimate stalker shoots and takes deer over a boundary or stalks on an area owned by absentee landlords. If caught, such poachers rely on the defence that they were retrieving a wounded beast or were simply mistaken over the boundary location.[131]

The B.S.E. crisis generated a need for traceability of animals and foodstuffs to allay public health concerns. With wild game it is not possible to develop such detailed systems and being a natural product, it is attractive to those seeking leaner, healthier meat. Whilst consumers are prepared to accept that venison is a wild product they also have a right to expect that when it comes under human control it is processed to the highest standards. Poached venison may never see a licensed game dealer or be subject to inspection and hygienic conditions. In many cases it is processed in the poacher's outhouse and it has been known for a carcase to be left hidden in a field for several days awaiting collection.

---

131. See chapter 7.

POACHING OFFENCES

The poacher does not differentiate between wild and captive deer. Venison is venison whether it is poached or stolen. However, as discussed in chapter 1, where captive deer are taken they are considered to have been not poached but stolen, and stronger legislation exists to deal with those responsible. Here we consider the taking of wild deer and we must look to the poaching offences in the Deer Acts north and south of the border and across the Irish Sea. The offences are similar in England, Wales, Northern Ireland and Scotland. Note, too, that the legislation applies equally to someone who has a right to be on the land, but not to take deer, such as a tenant, an employee or someone on a public right of way.

In England and Wales the legislation defines deer as deer of any species and includes the carcase and any part thereof. In Northern Ireland deer means deer of any species and their hybrids, and includes those on enclosed land, where deer not in the wild state are usually kept. In Scotland deer means fallow, red, roe and sika deer, and any other species specified in an order by the Secretary of State, and includes hybrids of those species, and where appropriate, the carcase of any deer or any part of it. So all species of deer are covered in England, Wales and Northern Ireland, while in Scotland only red, fallow, sika, roe and red/sika hybrids are specified plus any others specified by the Secretary of State.

England, Wales and Northern Ireland

Poaching is covered by the Deer Act, 1991 (section 22 of the Wildlife (Northern Ireland) Order, 1985, contains similar offences). Under section 1(1), it is an offence, without the consent of the occupier, owner or other lawful authority, to enter any land in search or pursuit of any deer with the intention of taking, killing or injuring it, and under section 1(2), it is an offence, without the consent of the occupier, owner or other lawful authority, while on any land, to:

- intentionally take, kill or injure any deer or attempt to do so
- search for or pursue any deer with such intent
- remove the carcase of any deer

Under section 1(3), however, a person will not be guilty under sections 1(1) or (2) if:

- he believes he would have had the owner's or occupier's consent if he had known of the circumstances
- he believed he had a lawful authority

Scotland

Under section 17 of the Deer (Scotland) Act, 1996, is it an offence:

- without legal right or permission to take, wilfully kill or injure deer on any land
- to remove the carcase of any deer from any land without legal right or permission from someone having such legal right
- to wilfully kill or injure any deer otherwise than by shooting with the prescribed firearm and ammunition

There is a view based on the game laws that where deer are legitimately shot on land where authority exists, but fall dead over the boundary, they can be recovered. There remain however, the issues of trespass and ownership of the carcase at civil law.[132]

Consent or permission

Consent is normally proved in a statement after the incident by establishing the rights to take deer. It is wise to record stalking arrangements, even informal ones, in writing. Informal, unrecorded agreements can result in doubts over consent, as with the stalker who claims permission was granted by a previous occupier.

Shooting or sporting contracts can be a source of confusion and dispute. In the 'good old days' gentlemen's agreements, written or made on a handshake, were often understood by the parties, but as time and individuals pass on problems arise. A typical situation is where an estate lets the sporting rights over a tenanted farm to a third party. The farm may later be sold to the tenant, who may then sell it to another person. Existing rights should be identified at the time of purchase by the solicitor who does the conveyancing, but new owners often take matters for granted and attempt to exercise rights which have been removed from the land, restricting access, setting up their own shoot, catching up birds or taking deer. There is no simple answer to such a problem. To prove consent or permission means looking at the contracts and sporting licence under the civil law.[133]

132. See chapters 7 and 8.
133. See chapter 1.

Location

The relevant piece of land has to be identified. This aspect is particularly important when the incident is close to a boundary and is normally proved by eye-witness evidence. Expert evidence may be used to disprove a claim that a shot deer ran over the boundary before falling dead.

Time limits

There are limits to the time that can elapse between the offence being committed and the taking of a prosecution. The general rule is a maximum of six months unless the legislation includes special provisions.

Trespass by a hunt

Section 35 of the Game Act 1831 provides that the offences of daytime poaching will not apply to a person lawfully hunting or coursing on any land with hounds or greyhounds, if in fresh pursuit of deer, hare or fox already started on other land.

However, although a poaching offence is not committed, there is still a civil trespass as section 35 does not give a hunt or anyone else the right to follow quarry onto another's land. The Game (Scotland) Act, 1832, contains similar provisions, but only in respect of fox and hare; the 1996 Deer (Scotland) Act prohibits the taking of deer by any other means than a legally permitted firearm and hunting with dogs is thus prohibited.[134]

Powers and penalties

The penalties for poaching are identical in all countries: on conviction a fine not exceeding level 4 on the standard scale and/or three months' imprisonment or both. The punishment can be applied to each deer taken. Powers to arrest and search vary, and they are covered in chapters 2 and 3.

OFFENCES ASSOCIATED WITH POACHING

The Deer Acts include numerous offences relating to illegal methods of taking deer, taking them at night and out of season, unlawful

---

134. See chapter 3.

firearms and the possession of illegal venison. Poaching offences may sometimes be difficult to prove, but there are many others which can be considered, which may carry a greater penalty. The most obvious are cruelty and vehicle-related offences, including driving while disqualified, drink driving and document offences.

Cruelty[135]

There is the possibility of proceedings under the Wild Mammals (Protection) Act, 1996 (England, Wales and Scotland). If someone, by his own actions or the use of a dog, mutilates, kicks, beats, nails, impales, stabs, burns, stones, crushes, drowns, drags or asphyxiates any wild mammal with intent to inflict unnecessary suffering he commits an offence. Any one of the above acts is sufficient and could easily be applied to deer poaching.

The Act was introduced following extreme acts of cruelty on wild mammals, notably nailing a vixen to a tree and using a hedgehog as a football. Before this Act wild mammals were not protected by the cruelty laws unless they were held in a state of captivity.

The Act contains exemptions which include:

- the humane dispatch of a disabled animal
- the humane and swift dispatch of an animal taken in the lawful course of shooting, hunting, coursing or pest control
- the lawful use of poison, a snare, trap, dog or bird for the purpose of killing or taking a wild animal

These exemptions only apply to *lawful* pursuits or the *lawful* use of certain methods. It follows therefore that activities which may be deemed unlawful, perhaps trespassing or acting without the owner's consent, may render someone liable to offences under this Act.

Driving on land (England, Wales and Scotland)

Under section 34 of the Road Traffic Act, 1988, it is an offence without lawful authority to drive a motor vehicle on common land, moorland, other land of any description not being part of a road, or on a public footpath or bridleway (except in emergencies or parking within 15 yards of a road). It is known for the police to dip the fuel tank for red diesel (fuel which is sold at a lower duty for non-road use). This is of great interest to Customs and Excise and often leads to the instant seizure of the vehicle and substantial penalties.

---

135. See also chapter 7.

Firearms offences[136]

These offences include:

- use of section 1 firearms contrary to certificate conditions
- possession of firearms by young persons
- trespass with a firearm – all types of firearms, even air weapons
- possession of a loaded firearm in a public place

Air weapons are also worth closer examination in case their power is such that they are classed as section 1 firearms. (Rifle exceeds 12ft/lb.)

Bows and crossbows are not classed as firearms but it is illegal to kill any bird or animal with them under the Wildlife and Countryside Act, 1981, in England, Wales or Scotland. In Northern Ireland it is illegal to take red, sika and fallow deer with any form of arrow.

Threats and intimidation

Encounters between poachers and deer managers are likely to result in threats and intimidation. Sometimes these may be directed at family members, homes, livestock and crops. Several pieces of legislation cover such behaviour, including the Public Order Act in England and Wales. Section 4 of this Act, for example refers to a person using towards another person threatening, abusive or insulting words or behaviour:

- with intent to cause that person to believe immediate violence will be used against him, or another, by any person
- with intent to provoke the immediate use of violence by the other person or another
- whereby that person is likely to believe that such violence will be used
- whereby it is likely that such violence will be provoked

Section 5 includes a person using threatening, abusive or insulting words or behaviour, or disorderly behaviour, within the hearing or sight of a person likely to be caused harassment, alarm or distress.

The offences can be committed in public or private places but not inside a house, and cater for confrontational situations. In a poaching situation, they apply equally to the gamekeeper and the poacher. It is necessary to prove the intent to create a fear of violence, harassment

136. See also chapter 6.

etc. which will rely on accurately recording the words and actions used by each individual. Only police officers have powers of arrest.

The intimidation of witnesses is covered by section 51 of the Criminal Justice and Public Order Act, 1994 (England and Wales), and similar offences apply in Scotland and Northern Ireland. The offence can be committed by any person who intimidates a person assisting in an investigation, a witness or juror. Threats need not be made in the presence of the person and may be financial as well as physical.

The Protection from Harassment Act, 1997 (the anti-stalking Act) contains offences of harassment and causing fear of violence.

Other offences

Criminal damage involves causing damage to buildings, fences, hedges, crops, captive or domestic birds or animals. It might include driving through hedges or across crops, injuring a keeper's dog or setting fire to buildings or haystacks.

Assault is the infliction of injury that amounts to severe bruising, cuts, broken bones or other discomforts.

Poachers may also be armed with **offensive weapons** or use an innocent object as a weapon when challenged. Under section 1 of the Prevention of Crime Act, 1953 (similar provisions apply in Scotland and Northern Ireland) it is an offence without reasonable excuse to have an offensive weapon in a public place. An offensive weapon is something made or adapted to cause injury, such as a baseball bat with a nail in it, a knuckle-duster or a cosh. It can also be anything which is used for the purpose – e.g. a walking stick or a hammer. Only the police can make an arrest.[137]

OBSERVATION AND IDENTIFICATION

Evidence requires an incident to be recorded from start to finish, and a written record, photograph, video or tape-recording are always more useful than your recollections. Always have a notebook and pen available to record details at the time or as soon as possible after the event – e.g. on return to your vehicle or when the police arrive. Tell the police about the notes, photographs, video or tapes to validate their authenticity.

The main principle of evidence-gathering is to present to a court the best evidence available – e.g. the actual carcase, the rifle or the

137. See chapter 7 for legislation governing the carrying of knives.

dog used by the poacher. There are obvious difficulties with some of these and a photograph is the next best thing. If a car number is written on a cigarette packet it becomes an exhibit and should be preserved and presented to the court as the best evidence.

It is vital that you note what each individual did and said. Identify each one by his clothing – e.g. the one in the wax jacket and the one in the cammo trousers. Who was driving? Who had the dog, the lamp, the gun? If vehicles were involved try to identify the driver, the vehicle, the road and locations where they were driven.

Intention and wilfulness

Proving intention or wilfulness is sometimes difficult. We do not know what is going through someone else's mind and must base our evidence on the poacher's actions or words. Seeing the kill, finding the poacher with a carcase, seeing a dog slipped on a deer under the lamp or a high-speed chase in a four-wheel-drive vehicle are often sufficient to prove intent. Finding a suspect walking the land with a gun or dog may not be enough – even if it is 3 a.m. It is better to observe him until his actions give him away. The comments on intention are also applicable to attempts to commit offences.

The search or pursuit element of the offences in England, Wales and Northern Ireland require similar evidence to that which proves intention. Many excuses can be given for the poacher's actions: 'I'm exercising the dogs', 'I'm only after rabbits', 'I'm walking on to land where I have the stalking' etc. Once again it is better to watch and wait until his actions prove his intentions.

Scientific evidence

Scientific evidence in the form of DNA, blood, bone or hair on clothing, dogs or vehicles, can connect a deer carcase taken from the land to a gralloch, amputated legs or head, or a pool of blood at

the scene. Knives and saws are also a source of flesh and bone fragments which can be compared with DNA from a carcase.

Videos

It is known for poachers to take photographs and videos of their activities which are often circulated amongst others with similar interests. Such evidence may be found in their vehicles but may also come to light when searching their homes for other evidence. Their activities often cause disgust amongst their friends and relatives who have been known to hand them in to the police.

Photographs or videos taken by a witness provide damning evidence and should be brought to the attention of the police at the earliest opportunity. Evidence as to the time, date and location of the filming will be covered in a witness statement. In many cases the police will take possession of the film and process it.

One difficulty, however, can be in establishing the date and the location of the incidents on film. Poachers may claim that the acts caught on film took place in another country where such activities are lawful. It may also be claimed that the incidents were several months or years old.

Continuity and identification

These two factors are important in the prosecution of any offence. Continuity has two main aspects:

- the recording and handling of exhibits
- evidence which proves a continuous, unbroken chain of events

The handling of all exhibits must be traced back to each person who has been involved at any stage in the proceedings. This is normally done by referring to them in a written statement. For example, if a gamekeeper writes down a car number on a scrap of paper and later hands the paper to a police officer who may then pass it on to other officers, the details must be recorded in a statement each time possession changes. Months later in court the chain of evidence can then track the paper from the gamekeeper to the court.

Another important aspect of continuity is the observation of suspects. Let us assume that in the middle of the night you see a lamp in a field next to a public footpath. In the beam you see a dog running towards a deer, then the lamp goes out. You make your way to the footpath and find a man with a dog and a lamp walking towards you. You may be convinced that they are the ones you saw in the field, but the chain of events is broken and you cannot legally connect the man on the path with the man in the field. The facts amount to circumstantial evidence which is not as strong as direct evidence. An unbroken chain would necessitate the tracking of the man from the field to the path.

Identification is another critical area which is challenged in court. Eye-witness evidence is subjected to several tests:

- the distance involved
- the lighting conditions and position of any street lamps
- the weather conditions
- whether the witness was wearing spectacles
- any obstructions between the witness and the suspect
- the time and duration of the observation
- whether the witness knew the suspect

YOUR STATEMENT

It is vital that your statement to the police contains not only the evidence but also your justification for spending court time and money on what may, to some people, appear to be a trivial matter. Your statement can influence the decision to prosecute and the penalties. A poaching case must pass two tests before it can get to court: there must be sufficient evidence to have a good chance of securing a prosecution, and it must be considered worthy of prosecution in the public interest.

Many poaching cases fail when the details which justify prosecution and subsequent penalties are not included in the statement. Do not expect the police, the Crown Prosecution Services and magistrates to know how deer are managed, the economics involved or the effects of poaching.

The following is a suggestion for the basis of your statement. It includes numerous options to cater for different circumstances and offences. Once you have described the situation on your estate you can use it as the basis of your statement in future cases.

> I am the [deer manager, stalker, gamekeeper, landowner, tenant, farmer, shooting tenant, etc.] in respect of land situated at [detail the area involved; consider providing an estate map].

Outline the responsibilities of the role, including:

- your employer (e.g. estate, syndicate, deer management group, forest owner)
- what you provide (e.g. stalking, trophies, venison production)
- who you provide it for (e.g. private owner, syndicate)
- how you do it (e.g. management by selective culling to promote healthy stock etc.)
- how you look after them (e.g. selective culling across an area in co-operation with other landowners, protection from poachers, night patrols etc.)
- if the estate is partly or wholly commercial what is meant by let days, stalking, trophies etc.
- how costs are calculated – what is charged per day, beats or trophy

Explain why you want the poachers prosecuted, including:

- the effect of poaching (an inability to provide the level of sport expected, the damage to stalking by disturbance the night before, loss of revenue, income tax and V.A.T., damage to the local economy in terms of income generated by way of equipment purchased, accommodation, food, etc., threat to employment, poor herd management)
- the public health risks from poached venison
- whether poaching affects proper deer management through indiscriminate killing
- the fact that poachers see a failure to prosecute as a sign of weakness, and that gamekeepers, their families and property are further exposed to violence, intimidation and financial loss
- why poaching is a problem in your locality

Describe what happened, including:

- what you saw and heard
- whether deer were injured or left to die
- whether livestock was worried or disturbed
- whether the poachers' acts were wilful – e.g. whether it was a gang from a city 100 miles away out to fill a van with venison or a couple of local youths taking pot shots with an air rifle, and whether there was any expression of regret
- if you were injured, details of injuries
- whether there were any threats of intimidation at the time or for the future and whether you have experienced any threats from these or other poachers in the past

COMPENSATION

Historically a realistic value has seldom been placed on fish, fur or feather and there has been a reluctance to claim compensation in poaching cases. Even in Roman times the principle of *ferae naturae* stated that wild animals were ownerless, but the right to take them has been jealously guarded through the centuries. Modern laws maintain this position on 'ownership' but rights to take sporting species remain enshrined in civil law. Sporting rights can change hands for vast sums of money and poaching can have a significant effect on the overall value of a piece of land.

The provision of sport for the leisure market has been phenomenal recently, and in many rural communities it is a financial lifeline through the jobs and money involved in providing accommodation, food, equipment and other local services. As we have said, you must assume that the police, magistrates, the Crown Prosecution Service and solicitors involved in a poaching case will be unaware of the significance to the local economy and the time, effort and investment which goes into a sporting estate – hence the detailed statement above.

Traditionally compensation has been based on the value of the venison at the game dealer's door but there is now an established legal authority for claiming compensation at the commercial value – Haslam v. C.P.S., Derby Crown Court, 1991. Although this case relates to poaching pheasants, its principles have been successfully applied to other species.

Haslam was found guilty of poaching thirty-six pheasants and the estate claimed the going rate at the time of £12 plus V.A.T. The keeper had to explain the process of managing an estate, of rearing and releasing birds into the wild, which he then tended by providing feed and protection from predators and poachers. Groups then rented out shooting by paying a fixed sum for each bird shot on the day. He explained what is obvious to those in the know: that birds were not released on the day of the shoot, so it was not possible to replace birds lost to poachers by buying in replacements from the game farm, and that such losses affected the number of birds which could be driven over the guns. Whilst there was no guarantee that the poached birds would have been shot and their value realised, the keeper drew a parallel with a baker, who does not sell all he bakes but must have bread for his customers to buy. The magistrates awarded £10 per bird, which went to the estate, in addition to a heavy fine for poaching and firearm offences.

It is difficult to apply a value to lamping hare and rabbit but you should be able to quantify the problems of poaching deer, in addition to the game and livestock, damage to fences, gates left open etc. For example, the stalking fee, trophy fee, carcase value, time taken to track an injured deer, potential damage to the herd.

In Derbyshire we successfully use a simple formula for the cost of poached trout: the total costs of running the club divided by the number of fish stocked. There are also figures available for rod-caught wild salmon, which often amount to several hundred pounds each.

The Haslam case has since been used successfully in other courts. Explain the grounds for your claim fully and include the following in your statement:

> I ask that compensation of . . . be awarded in accordance with Haslam v. C.P.S. Derby Crown Court, 1991, this being the value to my employer.

Here is a checklist for further action:

- Immediately after each incident write to the local police and the C.P.S. or Procurator Fiscal expressing your concerns.
- Emphasise that you wish to see a prosecution.
- Make a request for compensation.
- If you are able to attend court bring compensation to the notice of the C.P.S. prior to the start of the case.
- If you are injured ask for a Criminal Injuries Compensation form, even if the poacher was not arrested or identified.
- If you have concerns with the actions of the police or the prosecutor, write to the Chief Constable or head of the prosecution authority.

CITIZENS' ARREST

There may be situations when dealing with poachers where serious criminal offences are involved. In certain circumstances you may be empowered to make what is commonly referred to as a 'citizen's arrest'. These powers are contained in the Police and Criminal Evidence Act,1984. Such offences are known as 'arrestable offences', e.g.burglary, theft and damage. These types of crimes generally carry a prison sentence of at least 5 years.

Section 24(4) states that anyone may arrest someone who is, or you have *reasonable grounds* for suspecting is, in the act of committing an *arrestable offence*. The power also caters for a situation where you have not seen the offence committed but have reasonable grounds to suspect someone is guilty, provided you know an arrestable offence has been committed. So if you come across someone stealing deer from an enclosed deer farm or park, or damaging a high seat, then the persons responsible can be arrested.

Remember, the police have more extensive powers and are specifically trained to make arrests so as to minimise the risk to personal safety. If you get it wrong, not only may you suffer injury but you may be sued for false imprisonment.

CHAPTER 10

Poaching Prevention

The prevention of poaching is vital to all those who have a vested interest in the welfare of deer. Historically poaching prevention was an essential element of the gamekeeper's role and had an impact on the occasional deer poacher. But poaching trends have changed, and deer are now more likely to be poached than game birds.

Knowing how to deal with poachers, identify offences and gather evidence are all important but ideally our efforts should be concentrated on tactics to prevent it occurring in the first place. Prevention remains far better than cure. However, it is a difficult concept to get over to people who may not think they have a problem in the first place, even though their livelihood may depend on a sustainable level of quality deer. The danger is that once poachers have been successful in finding and taking deer in a particular area, it becomes difficult to stop repeated intrusions. They are after all, the ultimate opportunists, being able to pick their own time, place and method. They will have a good knowledge of the area and a well-rehearsed story should they be caught. Despite this, much can be done to bring successful prosecutions and prevent further poaching.

Deterrence or prosecution

You must decide whether you are prepared to tackle poachers with a view to a prosecution or simply to deter them by driving them off your land. For a prosecution to have a good chance it is often better to observe quietly, gather the evidence and step in after the kill. Trying to prove a poacher's intentions whilst in pursuit is more difficult and provides numerous excuses e.g. I was only exercising my dog and it ran after a deer—

To let the pursuit continue, however, may cause more damage by disturbing deer and livestock. In these circumstances it may be better to show a presence and get them off the land.

Making best use of law enforcement

The police have the primary responsibility for enforcing deer legislation and it is in their interests to apply resources effectively to its prevention and detection.

Instigating successful action through the courts where punishment can be imposed can be a useful deterrent, and as we have seen, raising the awareness of the Crown Prosecution Service and magistrates of the realities of poaching and its effect on rural communities is essential to successful prosecutions. This is strengthened if the right levels of compensation are applied for and full use is made of publicity.[138]

Where poaching problems exist liaison with the local police is essential, as your own powers to deal with such situations are weak.[139] All police forces have appointed wildlife liaison officers and whilst this responsibility is often ancillary to their normal duties they are a good point of contact and may well have considerable experience in dealing with poaching matters. If you do not know the local officers and need to establish contact you may write to your area divisional commander, who should put you in touch with the right people and ideally arrange a meeting locally, at which you can outline the problems. Such action raises the profile of deer poaching and can lead to a more positive approach from local officers at your time of need. A number of initiatives may be suggested, some of which are elaborated upon below.

138. See pages 184 and 190.
139. See chapters 2 and 3.

Alternatively you could contact the B.A.S.C. for their help and advice.[140] They have successfully campaigned against deer poaching as a rural crime for some years. Their aim has been to raise awareness of the economic, conservation and social implications of poaching in all its forms. They continue to work in partnership with the police to promote watch schemes and provide training and information.

The Crime and Disorder Act, 1998, requires local authorities and the police to work together with other key agencies and the community at local level to develop and implement strategies for reducing crime and disorder. In rural communities this may well involve strategies to reduce deer poaching. The first step involves reviewing the patterns and levels of crime and disorder by consulting widely with the local community. The strategies must be published and kept under review. This legislation is a very useful way forward in some rural areas, giving the police the necessary impetus to provide resources to combat poaching problems. The development of countryside watch schemes may be the type of initiative included in a strategy to reduce rural crime.[141]

It is apparent that much of our poaching law fails to prevent poaching. Even if poachers are stopped by the police and are equipped for such purposes, perhaps with a lamp and dogs, there may be little that can be done; a 'going equipped' offence does not exist. The practice of leaving the deer to be transported from the land the following day in commuter traffic, emphasises the inadequacy of the legislation.

Successful use has been made of legislation which is some 600 years old, known as the Justice of the Peace Act, 1361. The police in Dorset were faced with an unprecedented level of deer poaching and found they were powerless to deal with the situation because of the difficulty of actually catching the offenders in the act or with deer in their vehicles. Lamping deer at night had become very prevalent, particularly during the winter months. It was occurring over a wide area on a large scale, and was relatively well organised. Eventually some of the offenders were caught in possession of a number of deer carcases. Further enquiries revealed that they had been checked by the police on five separate occasions in the early hours of the morning on what were suspected to be journeys to or from poaching expeditions. Large lurcher-type dogs were seen in their vehicle and on one occasion a search revealed lamping equipment.

---

140. See page 203 for contact details.
141. See page 195.

In addition to charges under the Deer Act, proceedings by way of complaint were also taken under the Justice of the Peace Act, 1361. The magistrates were sufficiently convinced, in view of all the circumstances, that the defendants could well continue their poaching activities. Orders were made binding them over in the sum of £200 to keep the peace and be of good behaviour for a period of two years. The circumstances of this case emphasise the need for the efficient gathering of intelligence concerning the movements of poachers, their associates and activities, all of which should be properly recorded at the time.

This ancient law is thought to have been used to combat poaching in the reign of George I, when a poacher on the Duke of Beaufort's estate was compelled to enter a bond not to take game or fish there. In more recent years it has been used in respect of a variety of offences, including kerb crawling for prostitutes. There is however a reluctance to use such legislation to overcome the inadequacies of modern legislation.

Enforcement of the legislation relating to venison dealers is an important step in poaching prevention, and one that has been pioneered by the Devon and Cornwall Constabulary in their 'Operation Ostler'. This involved a force-wide initiative aimed at ensuring that licensed dealers complied with the Deer Act, 1991.[142] Working in partnership with dealers in this way was introduced to reduce the likelihood that poached venison would be traded and thereby reduce the incidents of poaching. The initiative involved a three-phase approach:

- liaison with the local authority to establish a comprehensive list of licensed dealers
- correspondence reminding dealers of their legal obligations
- random checks at their premises to inspect records and carcases

Using the media as a deterrent

The potential for positive coverage of poaching cases in the press is often high, and it can easily be encouraged by involving the media at an early stage. But you need to co-operate with them.

Over the years we have sought to dispel the myths of the romantic image of poaching and the issue of class associated with country sports. The media are now keen to portray poaching as a cruel pursuit which has a detrimental economic and environmental impact on rural

142. See chapter 5.

communities. Poachers are seen as criminals involved in a lucrative, illegal trade rather than as people taking from the rich to feed the poor.

The involvement of the media must be a benefit; they need a good story that will generate interest, and you need the exposure to deter poaching. But there are also risks. You may draw attention to the presence of deer in an area which was previously little known, and thereby attract unwelcome interest from a variety of sources, including poachers. However we believe the advantages of 'going public' outweigh the risks.

TV reporters will often need first-hand accounts by video interview. This may not be as daunting as you imagine and the interview not normally 'live'; if you make an error it can be done again. They will not want to rehearse matters with you too much, as this tends to spoil the spontaneity of the interview, but you should first check out the general areas of interest. Remember that they will not have first-hand knowledge of the issues and you should advise them accordingly. If you have a message to put across in the interview, for example inviting viewers to report suspicious incidents, then ensure that there is an opportunity for you to do so.

They will want to film the location if possible and any deer that may have been taken, and possibly at short notice. However, if a case is to go to court, the matter will be *sub judice* and any information or material must not be published until after the court proceedings. This is not unusual and should not be a bar to your co-operation, but you should seek the advice of the police officer dealing with the case.

Dealing with the media may be inconvenient, but the deterrent factor should not be underestimated. It is a valuable and powerful weapon in combating poaching by the exposure of antisocial behaviour and cruelty towards deer. Public interest is raised and may ultimately influence how such matters are viewed by the courts.

Physical deterrents

Unfortunately, for many poachers the thought of capture and conviction is a wholly inadequate deterrent compared to the sheer excitement and financial gains of further nightly raids. You need to concentrate on making your estate or stalking area a hard target. There are a number of practical measures you can take to achieve this.

First you must assess the level of poaching and how it is being done. If this is not known but you suspect it is likely, then consider the methods described on page 193. A key deterrent in lowland areas is

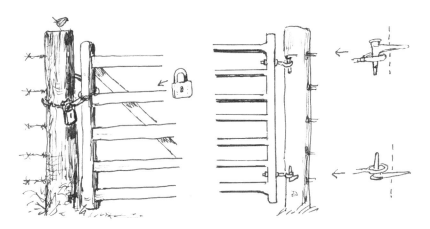

Restrict access by securing gates.

to restrict vehicular access. Basic security can be relatively inexpensive and quite effective. You should restrict access to vehicles as far as possible in vulnerable areas – mainly those adjacent to the public roads or easily accessible from them. Closing and locking gates to private roads or access to fields is particularly important and wherever possible they should be chained and locked. Hedgerows and fences should be maintained and where they do not exist you should consider other means of preventing vehicular access. Many landowners have access to heavy plant which could be used to create small trenches at points where access would otherwise be easily gained by 4x4 vehicles.

In remote highland areas, where it is more common for deer to be poached by shooting from the road or taking to the hill on foot with a rifle, prevention is more difficult. In these situations good intelligence and observation are essential, with heavy covert patrolling. If it is well co-ordinated with the police, this enables suspects to be stopped and searched at strategic locations.

Night-time surveillance is essential and can have a psychological effect on would-be poachers if they become aware that they have been seen. Gamekeepers have always practised 'night watching' in the past, and know its value as a deterrent. It involves active patrolling in the areas you consider most at risk. Good police liaison is essential and it is advisable to have established links with local officers prior to your night patrols. Record times and places where fences are damaged or vehicle tracks left, so that you know when there has been an unwanted presence on the land. This intelligence can then be used to target your patrols effectively. Good intelligence of the movements

of suspected poachers and their vehicles is vital. Ideally you should have a system of communication by which information can be quickly circulated.

Vehicles are not always to be found discreetly hidden in gateways or farm tracks; you should bear in mind that where urban development is close by they may be left in pub car parks or secreted between residents' vehicles on housing estates. It is far more likely that poachers will not have left their vehicle and will be on the move, looking for areas to drive onto and lamp deer actually on the move. In the Highlands they may drive into remote areas with rifles on board ready to shoot from the vehicle if the opportunity presents itself. It is a difficult situation to deal with, as you do not have power to stop or search such vehicles on the road, even if you have previously seen them involved in poaching on the land. This power is restricted to the police and you must be content with circulating the intelligence quickly and hoping that they may be stopped and searched by them.

Pursuing a poacher's vehicle on the public road is fraught with danger and should be avoided at all costs. You should content yourself with the knowledge that the poachers will know they have been seen and that their activities have been obstructed. You should have a good practical knowledge of your legal powers[143] and should guard against the temptation to act outside them. To do so will render you liable to counter-claims and actions through the criminal or civil courts.

---

143. See chapters 2 and 3.

If you are dealing with poachers at night you should involve the police early, when your suspicions are first raised. This is particularly important when you suspect firearms are involved. You should maintain observations from a safe distance until assistance arrives. Only police officers have powers to seize firearms and make arrests in respect of deer poaching, so improving police liaison and the setting up of watch schemes is a key element of your prevention tactics. Poachers quickly get to know the estates and areas where keepers and deer managers are active and vigilant. They do not like being watched or their whereabouts being noted. Eventually they will either be caught or go elsewhere, into areas which are not so well policed.

Daytime vigilance and the value of observation

Maintaining vigilance during the day can be rewarding. It is common for poachers to undertake reconnaissance prior to night-time activities, and this type of intelligence can be invaluable. If you can see deer in the hot spots from the road, then so can the poachers. You may be able to move them or discourage them from visiting these visible areas. In crime prevention parlance this would be known as 'target hardening'.

It is a well-known practice for deer poachers to hide carcases in the night and return the next day when suspicions may not be aroused. A vehicle you think is a courting couple or a family on a picnic could be collecting the previous night's spoils. If you find a carcase you suspect has been hidden by poachers you should involve the police in any observations you mount, in the hope of the culprits returning. You must remain discreet in your activities and plans. Our experience in these situations suggest that observations can be worthwhile provided sufficient police resources are allocated. The legislation provides for offences of removing carcases from land.[144]

Two cases in Derbyshire emphasise the value of mounting such observations. The first involved a gamekeeper who found a fallow buck hidden in bracken, apparently shot with either a .22 or a crossbow. The police were involved and a decision taken to keep observation on the carcase that evening. As darkness fell three men arrived and attempted to remove the beast to a nearby vehicle. They were arrested and taken to the local police station before they had an opportunity to agree a line of defence. When they were interviewed the first man said his dog had accidentally chased and killed the beast.

144. See chapters 2 and 3.

The second man said it was a mercy killing, as they had found the beast in a bad way caught in some baler twine. And the third man said, 'What deer?' The magistrates subsequently found all three guilty of removing a carcase from land.

The second incident highlights the need for patience and determination in obtaining evidence. A mature red stag had been brutally killed within the enclosed deer park of a stately home now owned by the National Trust. Part of the carcase was discovered, hidden in undergrowth and observations were kept for two days, but without success. The part-carcase was removed. On the third day a vehicle was seen in the vicinity in suspicious circumstances and details circulated to the police. The vehicle was later stopped and searched some miles from the scene of the incident. To the officer's surprise, he found not only cutting equipment but part of the original red deer carcase taken on the night. The driver was arrested on suspicion of *theft* as the deer, having been taken from enclosed land, was treated as having been stolen rather than poached.[145] At court the man stated he had come by the venison innocently, having purchased it as dog meat from a man he had met in a lay-by. He was subsequently convicted of handling stolen property under the Theft Act, 1968.

Countryside watch schemes

Setting up poacher or deer watch schemes involving the police, landowners, keepers and stalkers can be extremely effective. Such schemes are not new and have had considerable success throughout the country. They are more successful if they involve the support of the wider community, not just those with an interest in deer. An essential element is the gathering, exchange and circulation of intelligence on suspected poachers, their vehicles, methods, and movements.

Other aspects of such schemes should include the determination of well-defined rendezvous points and the issue of standardised maps to all parties which clearly indicate boundaries and relevant information. Good communications are essential and can be achieved by the use of personal radios or mobile telephones. The latter are particularly useful where help is required urgently. The ability to ring for assistance from a remote area of woodland is an invaluable asset.

Remember that poachers have access to communication equipment, including radios on which they have been known to monitor other transmissions. Therefore in planning your operations you

145. See chapter 1.

should include codes for identification and locations and supply relevant maps.

Watch schemes tend to encourage co-operation between neighbouring estates, which can be of mutual benefit. The pooling of resources affords greater personal safety, mobility and effectiveness. Night-vision equipment, although expensive, can give you the upper hand. By syndicating the purchase and use of such equipment the cost can be considerably reduced. There are a number of practical measures you can take, all of which contribute to making your area a hard target.[146] Basic security considerations are essential, particularly those restricting vehicular access points in vulnerable areas.

Let it be known that you are using night-vision equipment, radios etc. Publicise the watch scheme and the use of joint patrols. A high-powered lamp sweeping across a valley or along a wood side can be quite effective in demonstrating your presence. If you are short handed, carry two lamps each. Take the initiative; you have the advantage of local knowledge and assistance.

Watch meetings are key events that members should be encouraged to attend. They should be about developing future strategy rather than wasting time on anecdotal criticisms of the scheme or the police's response. Positive outcomes of such meetings include the opportunity to socialise, and presentations on associated topics such as law or deer management. A raffle in aid of a local charity also provides a good media opportunity.

Data protection

If you decide to organise a watch scheme or are already involved in one then you should be aware of the restrictions imposed by the Data Protection Acts of 1984 and 1998. There may be liabilities if you are involved in the circulation of intelligence concerning poachers.

The Acts give legal rights to individuals in respect of personal data held about them by others and places obligations on those who process information about individuals. The latter must be open about the use to which the information is put (through the data protection register) and follow sound and proper practices (the data protection principles). The legislation protects an individual's right to privacy and provides safeguards on the way personal information is used.

Unless a watch scheme is able to fulfil the conditions attached to an exemption from registration, it will need to register its intentions to process personal data.

However, having due regard for data protection and other legal

146. See page 191.

obligations, the police may disclose limited details to watch schemes for the prevention or detection of crime. Such details will not normally be deemed 'personal data' within the terms of the Acts.

Where information such as the details of suspicious vehicles are circulated, it should be made clear that care must be taken in the subsequent use of that information, in that it may no longer be accurate. The vehicle may now be driven quite legitimately or have changed ownership. There is a good deal that can be circulated without the need for registration. Clearly personal details such as a poacher's name and address would contravene the Acts unless registration had been granted. But a watch scheme could circulate the following type of information, for example, without liability:

> Between 2 a.m. and 4 a.m. on Sunday, 4 January, the following vehicle was seen in the Peak Forest area in suspicious circumstances. Occupants are suspected of deer poaching. Toyota four-wheel-drive, red colour, registered number ABC 123D. The vehicle was seen to contain two white youths, both with short cropped hair and a number of lurcher-type dogs.

If you keep details of persons involved in the scheme, such as a fellow keeper or landowner, you may share information, but ensure that individuals know what is to be done with their personal information and that you gain their consent. You should only collect information that you can justify for the purposes of the scheme.

The registrar's staff are happy to assist with any queries you may have and can be contacted at the Office of the Data Protection Registrar, Wycliffe House, Water Lane, Wilmslow, Cheshire SK9 5AF.

List of Statutes

List of Cases

Bibliography

Chapman, Norma : *Deer*, Whittet Books
Chapman, Norma : *Fallow Deer*, The Mammal Society
Smith J.C. : *The Law of Theft*, Butterworth
Everitt, Nicholas : *Shots from a Lawyer's Gun*, Gilbertson and Page Ltd
Haigh J.C. : *Deer Magazine*, Vol. 10, No. 3
Stair Memorial Encyclopaedia, Vol. 11. 'Game'
Sandys-Winsch, B.A. Godfrey : *Animal Law*, Shaw & Sons
Sandys-Winsch, B.A. Godfrey : *Gun Law*, Shaw & Sons
Riddall, J.G. : *Land Law*, Butterworth
Riddall & Trevelyan : *Rights of Way – a guide to law and practice*, Ramblers'
  Ass.
Highways Agency : *The Prevention of Casualties Amongst Deer Populations*
  S.W.335/V2/08-97 Aug 1997
Radford, Mike : *Animal Cruelty and the Courts*, Justice of the Peace, Vol.
  162
Chenevix-Trench, Charles : *The Poacher and the Squire*, Longmans
Mead, Lawrence : *Oke's Game Laws*, Butterworth
Smith & Hogan : *Criminal Law*, Butterworth
Nature Conservancy Council : *The Capture and Handling of Deer*
Stranks, Jeremy : *Health & Safety Law*
Halsbury's Laws of England, 3rd ed.
Parkes, Charlie & Thornley, John : *Fair Game*, Pelham Books
Parkes, Charlie : *Law of the Countryside*, Countryside Management
  Association
Whitehead, G. Kenneth: *The Whitehead Encyclopaedia of Deer*, Swan Hill
  Press

Whitehead, G. Kenneth : *Half a Century of Scottish Deer Stalking* Swan Hill Press

Prior, Richard : *Roe Stalking*, Game Conservancy Ltd

Prior, Richard : *Modern Roe Stalking*, Tideline Books

Adams, John & Dannatt, Norman : *The Culling and Processing of Deer*

LACOTS : *Wild Game, Guidance on Recommended Standards for Wild Game*

Deer Commission for Scotland : *Codes of Practice for Driving and Night Shooting of Deer*. Policy for Sika Deer

Stones Justice's Manual: Butterworths

Wignall, Gordon : (August 1998) 'Handling nuisance claims', *Solicitors Journal*

Harwood, Michael : (June 1995) 'Litigation', *Solicitors Journal*

Lord Cullen : *Report of the Public Enquiry into the Shooting at Dunblane Primary School*

Bateson, P. : (1997) *The Behavioural and Physiological Effects of Culling Red Deer*, London: The National Trust

Broadbent, Graham : (August 1993) 'Problems with knives', *Justice of the Peace* Magazine

Warlow, T. A. : *Science and Justice* 1996

Frost, David : *Sporting Firearms and the Law*, Countryside Alliance

Archbold : *Criminal Pleading, Evidence & Practice*, 1999. Sweet & Maxwell

Useful Addresses and Contacts

British Association for Shooting and Conservation
Marford Mill
Rossett
Wrexham
LL12 0HL

British Deer Society
Burgate Manor
Fordingbridge
Hampshire
SP6 1EF

Northern Ireland Deer Society
Laurel Bank
Rugby Avenue
Newry Road
Banbridge
Co. Down
BT32 3NA

Deer Commission for Scotland
Knowsley
82 Fairfield Road
Inverness
IV3 5LH

English Nature
Northminster House
Peterborough
PE1 1UA

Scottish Landowners' Federation
25 Maritime Street
Edinburgh
EH6 5PW

**The U.K. Association of
Professional Deer Managers**
PO Box 372
Exeter
EX5 5YL

**Humane Slaughter
Association**
The Old School
Brewhouse Hill
Wheathampstead
Hertfordshire
AL4 8AN

**British Wild Boar
Association**
38 Spring Street
London
W2 1JA

**National Game Dealers'
Association**
38 Spring Street,
London
W2 1JA

*Shooting Times and Country
Magazine*
King's Reach Tower
Stamford Street
London
SE1 9LS

Stalking Magazine
Field Sport Publications Ltd
PO Box 372
Exeter
EX5 5YL

Forestry Commission
Great Eastern House
Tenison Road
Cambridge
CB1 2DU

The Game Conservancy
Fordingbridge
Hampshire
SP6 1EF

**British Shooting Sports
Council**
PO Box 11
Bexhill on Sea
East Sussex
TN40 1ZZ

**Country Landowners'
Association**
16 Belgrave Square
London
SW1X 8PQ

Countryside Alliance
The Old Town Hall
367 Kennington Road
London
SE11 4PT

**Firearms Consultative
Committee**
50 Queen Anne's Gate
London
SW1H 9AT

Royal Ulster Constabulary
Firearms Licensing Branch
Linasharragh
Montgomery Road
Belfast

Royal Ulster Constabulary
Firearms Licensing Department
Knocknagoney House
Knocknagoney Road
Belfast
BT4 2PP

Department of Justice
Firearms Section
72-76 St Stephen's Green
Dublin

Customs Directorate Division
Import of Firearms
Branch C
12th Floor
Alexander House
21 Victoria Avenue
Southend on Sea
SS9 1AD

Export Licensing Unit
Department of Trade and
Industry
Kingsgate House
66-74 Victoria Street
London
SW1E 6SW

RSPCA
Causeway
Horsham
Sussex
RH12 1HG

British Deer Farmers' Association
Old Stoddah Farm
Penruddock
Penrith
CA11 0RY

LACOTS; Local Authorities Co-ordinating Body on Food and Trading Standards
PO Box 6
Robert Street
Croydon
CR9 1LG

John Adams and Norman Dannatt
Arun District Council
Civic Centre
Maltravers Road
Littlehampton
Sussex
BN17 5LE

Ministry of Agriculture, Fisheries and Food
Animal Health Division III
Hook Rise South
Tolworth
Surbiton
Surrey
KT6 7DX

Index